VIA Folios 103

Songs of The Sparrow
The Poetry of Felix Stefanile

Felix Stefanile

BORDIGHERA PRESS

Library of Congress Control Number: 2014944617

© 2015 by Selma Stefanile

All rights reserved. Parts of this book may be reprinted only by written permission from the author, and may not be reproduced for publication in book, magazine, or electronic media of any kind, except for purposes of literary reviews by critics.

Printed in the United States.

Published by
BORDIGHERA PRESS
John D. Calandra Italian American Institute
25 West 43rd Street, 17th Floor
New York, NY 10036

VIA FOLIOS 103
ISBN 978-1-59954-080-1

This compilation of poetry books is dedicated to the memory of their author, Felix Stefanile, whose elegance and eloquence were second to none, and who never held it over anyone.

A mentor, and yet a friend first, Felix's generosity of spirit shall be forever appreciated and never forgotten.

— *The Editors*, Bordighera Press

TABLE OF CONTENTS

Preface   ix

River Full of Craft   1
The Patience That Befell   59
A Fig Tree in America   73
East River Nocturne   159
In That Far Country   225
The Dance at St. Gabriel's   257
The Country of Absence   343

Afterword, by Dana Gioia   413

Index of Poems and Essays   421

Preface

This compilation of Felix Stefanile's poetry books is comprised of all seven volumes he published during his lifetime. Given Felix's propensity to publish with what was once called small presses, which today some often call "boutique" presses, many of these books may no longer be in print, and, as a result, the later generations of readers and poets would find it most difficult to find them.

In order to preserve the integrity of his trajectory, we decided to publish each book in its entirety, even if it meant repeating poems in subsequent collections. The only changes are the page numbers in each book's table of content, where we decided to use the page numbers of this collective volume. Otherwise, each book is reproduced as it was first published, including its original front matter. That said, the reader will find some table of contents and titles of poems in capital letters, in italics, and/or both. Also, in the two collections that did not have a table of contents, *In That Far Country* and *The Patience That Befell*, we decided to respect Felix's original idea of not including one.

※

When Felix Stefanile died at the age of 88, January 27, 2009, both America and Italian America lost one of its great poets, translators, and thinkers.

Felix was born April 13, 1920, in Long Island, NY, to the late Frank Stefanile and Genevieve Lauri Giannicchi. Educated in the New York school system in the 1920s and 1930s, he received his bachelor's degree from the College of the City of New York, of The City University of New York, in 1944.

A veteran of World War II, Felix served as an interpreter for the U.S. Army and went on to co-author a manual on how to fight malaria in Southern Italy. After the war, he worked at various jobs until 1950, when he took a position with the New York State Department of Labor until 1961. During that time, he and his wife Selma (nee Epstein, whom he married in 1953, and who has been instrumental in getting this collection published), a poet in her own right, started *Sparrow* (1954), which remained one of the oldest poetry journals in the United States, until they stopped publication in 2000. They founded the journal "to lead the life of poetry"; it was their "idiosyncratic odyssey." Over the years, *Sparrow* steered itself toward form, specifically the sonnet. In explaining such a move, Felix responded as follows to Gloria G. Brame in a 1994 interview: "I love the sonnet; I'm devoted to it.... It's also an air-tight editorial alibi.... Furthermore, it's a form that is a paradigm of the genuine writing experience: closure, constraint, contrast, accuracy of expression, focus, architectonics of syntax."

Felix won numerous awards for his poetry, essays, and teaching. In 1966 he penned an essay entitled "The Imagination of the Amateur," which earned him a National Endowment for the Arts prize in 1967. In 1973, he was awarded the prestigious Standard Oil of Indiana Prize for best teacher at Purdue University and in 1997 he was the first recipient of the John Ciardi Award for lifetime achievement in poetry, presented by the journal *Italian Americana*.

During his long and distinguished career, Felix authored a plethora of essays in the best journals in the United States and abroad, numerous books of poetry and translated some of Italy's finest poets, from the middle ages to the twentieth century. His books of poetry and translations include: *A Fig Tree in America* (New Rochelle, NY: Elizabeth Press, 1970); *East River Nocturne* (New Rochelle, NY: Elizabeth Press, 1976); *Indiana, Indiana: A Local Reader*, edited by Felix and Selma Stefanile (West Lafayette, Ind.: Sparrow Press, 1976); *Umberto Saba, Thirty-one Poems*, translations by Felix Stefanile (New Rochelle, NY: Elizabeth Press, 1978); *In That Far Country* (West Lafayette, Ind.: Sparrow Press, 1982); *The*

Blue Moustache: Some Futurist Poets, translations by Felix Stefanile (New Rochelle, NY: Elizabeth Press 1980); *If I Were Fire: Thirty-Four Sonnets by Cecco Angiolieri,* translated by Felix Stefanile (Iowa City: Windhover Press at the University of Iowa, 1987); *The Dance at St. Gabriel's* (Brownsville, OR: Story Line Press, 1995); *The Country of Absence: Poems and an Essay* (West Lafayette, Ind.: Bordighera, 2000).

Felix moved to Purdue University in 1961 as a visiting poet and lecturer. After that initial year, he was asked to stay on as a member of the English Department, and in 1969, he was appointed full professor. He retired from Purdue in 1987, the year we first met him. In the subsequent thirteen years Felix and Selma became dear friends in one sense, mentors in another. Possessing profound intelligence, affable wit, and a wonderful gift of language, Felix proved ever generous in spirit and consul. His wisdom was infinite, and he dispensed it charitably; his erudition was extensive, and he shared it willingly. One could not expect any more from such a bountiful and integral human being. For those of us who came to know him well, we are forever the beneficiaries of his munificence and magnanimity.

In exhorting his Italian/American sisters and brothers to learn of their history, he once stated: "There is no ontology without archaeology!" Felix always knew how to say what had to be said. He stated as much, in the early 1990s, during a discussion on Italian Americana at one of Purdue University's annual conference on Romance Languages, Literatures, and Film. Let us now follow his advice, and example, and pick up our books and learn even more

We miss him dearly!

※

This volume appears five years after Felilx's passing. In Italian, five years constitute a "lustro"; the English translation is "luster" or "shine." Thus, Felix's poetry, as well as the legacy of elegance he leaves us, shall indeed continue to shine for future poets and readers of verse. Felix always led by example. Now, his writing (poetry, essays, and translations) shall continue that lead for all to follow.

We wish to thank, first of all, Selma Stefanile, who accepted our idea of this project without hesitation and has helped us bring it to fruition. We also need to thank members of our editorial team, Rebecca Rizzo, Lisa Cicchetti, and Deborah Starewich, who was there at the beginning when we learned much from Felix,.

If Bordighera Press and our journal, *Voices in Italian Americana*, have had any good fortune along the way, it is because both Felix and Selma were there at the beginning, offering us indispensable advice on so many aspects of this delightful and, yet at time, challenging enterprise.

This is indeed for Felix!

Fred L. Gardaphe
Paul A. Giordano
Anthony Julian Tamburri
EDITORS, BORDIGHERA PRESS

Songs of The Sparrow

RIVER FULL OF CRAFT

POEMS

FELIX STEFANILE

RIVER FULL OF CRAFT

Poems

FELIX STEFANILE

PUBLISHED BY THE NEW ORLEANS POETRY JOURNAL
New Orleans, Louisiana
November 1956

Copyright, 1956, by Felix Stefanile

All rights reserved under U.C.C.

My sincerest thanks are due to those editors and magazines which first published the poems appearing in this book, and I now gratefully acknowledge this: *American Weave, The Beloit Poetry Journal, The Bridge, Civ/n, Discovery No. 4, Epos, Experiment, Flame, New Mexico Quarterly, New Orleans Poetry Journal, Poetry: A Magazine Of Verse, The Poet, The Poetry Chap Book, The Poetry Book Magazine, Voices,* and the anthology, *Eight American Poets.*

G.G. AND S.S.
This book is for my mother, and my wife:

Al cor gentil ripara sempre Amore
— Guido Guinizelli

CONTENTS

I. CITY OF IRON METAPHORS

As I Went Out One Morning	9
The Afternoon as an Aria	11
The Marionettes	12
A Late Elegy for a Baseball Player	15
Fioretti:	16
This Suicide	17
An Old Bootblack in the Cafeteria	19
East River Nocturne	20
Bal Tabarin	21
The Doge's Palace	23
Song	25

II. EYE

A Domestic Notion, for Selma	29
The Eye	30
Spoiled by All My Tyrants	31
Brown, All of the Autumn	32
In the Sea's Alchemies	33
To Wish	34
Calm Day	35
Elegy for My Father	37
Village on My Back	38
Feast of San Gennaro	39
Color and Line	40

III. SCENES FOR A LIGHT OPERA

An Old Reunion	43
I Fond Me a Lover	44
Fall of Adam	45

Scene for a Light Opera ... 46
Days Which Enchant Us ... 47
Malespina ... 49
Winter Year ... 51
The Leave-Taking ... 53
Spiaggia ... 54
Insomniac ... 56

THAT UNDERGROUND SUN ... 57

CITY OF IRON METAPHORS

AS I WENT OUT ONE MORNING

As I went out one morning
to take the pleasant air,
lolly too dum too dum lolly too dum day,

alephs and beths and
ghimels of lamentation
showered from the trees
and chirped on the iron fences,
and the Philip of me went strolling by
in search of his own lameness.

Up the avenue
and down the town, pink children
played at baseball and jacks and murder.
I laughed at an ugly woman:
from the rhetoric of her scorn
I limped to my repentance.

And as I went out one morning
to take the pleasant air,

just as I went strolling by
the shopwindows displayed John's head
lolly too dum day,
and a boy with the lungs of conscience
offered me false headlines
screaming Armistice towards Love,

and then, in the pleasant air,
all the mailmen hurried from me,
shielding their bags that never hold
news of emerald raffles in heaven:
only the same bony town,
Christ on his twigs, the devil
to his Marguerite, and lolly

too

THE AFTERNOON AS AN ARIA

The afternoon was an aria from Verdi;
the strolling cop beat time with casual club,
and the statues, courteous in stone,
dreamed in the humming shadows of the park.

The breeze was a nickelodeon of pigeons
and I called to my girl by the railing
come my lovely, away from those stone benches,
and dream with me of a prefab in the sky —

a duplex with green shutters, and furnished with squirrels,
and you, my little wife, in a silver kitchen,
frying me bacon and gold,
while I, with a brand-new pipe, stand by the varnished mailbox,
gently murdering salesmen on the lawn.

THE MARIONETTES

See how they dream their wooden dreams:
Oak legends are in their painted eyes.
Their ardor is of crepe and chalk.
The fire is their only surprise.

Catch how they mouth their gargoyle talk;
they even love with a scratching sound.
The fire is their only surprise,
Pinocchio burning himself to the ground.

Watch how they dance their clacking dance;
their kiss is like the breaking of a box.
They would sprout leaves like fingers of sense—
Master Gepetto, how they dance,

sauntering past with chirping knees
through the proscenium's feast of eyes,
wanting, perhaps, not to be made of wood.
The fire is their only surprise.

City of iron metaphors,
the children applaud their angular pranks
as their freak noses bump in fiction.
Do they hope that mothers will offer thanks?

See how they turn their necks of bark,
wound and wired for noise and friction.
They are not muddy children lost in the dark.
The fire is their only surprise.

Friend Cricket, your ardent piccolo
weeps from the wall like a prophecy.
They are so lonely racked upon the shelves.
They can weep splinters if only they try.

They're not content to be their wooden selves,
plotting a vegetable jacquerie
with their sinister sonorous Italian names
dreaming some varnished mythology.

Friend-Cricket, you bug-christ on the wall,
Pinocchio, brother to the Cross,
murdered you twice, with hammer and stick.
They are all cousins to Joan's sake.

The fire is their only surprise.
They love a green and yellow courtesan
with a silver dress and amber eyes.
The moon is their favorite citizen.

And all unsteadied by their pilgrimage
to this lost season, like a sleeping town
visited by their pushcart prompt parades,
I spy a hundred wooden strangers in the lemon dawn

shouting I love you in their fey dialects,
their chatterbox tarantellas waking the glades:
Columbina, the barking of Melampo,
toy apples of Giuseppina's breasts,

coming back from the ultimate thules of illusion,
and Puncinello, staring with eyes of pearl,

singing I love the child with the blue hair,
I love the green and yellow girl.

THE LATE ELEGY FOR A BASEBALL PLAYER

He was all back,
his stance was clumsy,
ran like a horse,
smiled with a dimple,
but Time cut him,
as easy as that,

bowled him right over,
muscle and all, for
a crick in his honest back—
the well-wrought stallion,
cleats on his shoes,
and a hometown shoulder,

full of country bumps.
We read about Herakles,
And the hairy Samson,
and fake Olympic games:
the whole world boos;
but here's Big Lou

whom Death bowled over
as the sun rose,
a lazy foul ball,
and a whole generation
of the running boys
pull up, cry loud,

at what Death caught.

FIORETTI:

For Sherwood Anderson and for his town.
(Americans invade America.)
He watched our mortal gods go flip! and drown
in meadowseas, in amber boarding-rooms

touched by a homesick prairie sun, in banks
not run by poets. He was very tall.
For Malatesta also I give thanks:
A crazy anarchist no enemy dared kill

for fear the ports of Europe would explode.
They kept him like a trophy in his house,
the gardeners his guards, while from the road
people saw, and wondered but were dumb.

Aware of a peculiar victory,
for Pete the barber, too: with his guitar
ignoring business while he played. A flea
to itch my conscience and scatter my mongrel-pride.

For Guido Cavalcanti, Waller too —
slow voice and fast guitar on the evening air —
immortal insolence of their art and love:
to bid a song, a rose, to go somewhere.

THIS SUICIDE

This suicide earned his agony like a coin:
morrows of marauders no longer will come.
Though the murdered years refuse him kingdom,
he'll sleep in the private oceans of the moon,
returning like a Ulysses of the womb.

His was the drama of a penny tempest:
where destiny, wearing her war like an opera gown
invaded the clinics of the city's passion
to spill his laureate veins, hid dripping vest,
on the tattered table some alderman had invested
with the trick biology of public eucharist.

He must have welcomed the fingers of the student
squeaking his heart that swelled in him like a grape.
Fruit of his dreams had grown in an Eden of apes,
till he sipped, in the cafeterias of our most prudent,
that one immortal coffee to keep him awake
tracing a tryst with Poseidon and his trident.

Now stevedores heaving the blue junk of empire
will loathe the reluctant thievery of his death.
Though men are democrats at a midday beer,
they will turn Nero vomiting a fat youth
to learn that so thin a one had no fear of breath,
and raped his failure as if she were most fair.

And now he smiles, I think, out of all anguish,
to know at last the esteem in which we held him—

tax, tithe and ticket, and the pretty onrush
of reporter who never knew him, but now have belled him
with tiger notes, that tell in a gaudy language
of how he died. But not of how we failed him.

AN OLD BOOTBLACK IN THE CAFETERIA

I watch him stumble into the place,
dragging his speech behind him like a limp,
shuffling up to the counter next to me
to beg a coffee with the dimes of his eyes.

There is about him no humility:
his jigging muscles hold his chin alert
as if to face life's blows, an exiled king
from a shoeshine country, dirty, but full of heart.

Placing a fist on the glass, he seems to sing
the news of his presence to an ignorant crowd,
waiting with a moan as plain as a hymn
for the boy with the Western accent to bring food.

And I catch the smiles they exchange, like prisoners
meeting in a dingy jail in a lean year:
a homesick boy, an old man crooked with age
carrying his coffee like a piece of fame

to where he sits beside the busy doors,
his strapped box set by him like a toy fort
stacked with the ammunition of his waste.
And as is passes, speaks to the World's shoes.

EAST RIVER NOCTURNE

The river turns and worries at my dreams,
waking me with the knowledge that the night
is filled with trophies, and how in the cobbled streets
the stones shine like new medals,
and the wharves
bear gulls like peacocks to the river's edge.

And the turning river worries at my dreams
till I grow fearful of the headlight moon
that flashes on a warehouse like a burglar,
filling my room with a laughter that shines
but is silent.

And I am sleepless, and beggar after nightmare
to shake the shine and shudder of a dirty river,
reading a morning meaning in the dead billboards
that drift like barges out of Egypt on the water.

BAL TABARIN

Disdain is mutual. We face the bar
an antique afternoon, when the raphaelite curve
of her smooth cheek is amber to my woe.
Time is expensive, fragrant as a rose.
true worshipper, I've come to kill my gods
a chilly easter, ardent to the last
season of enemies, and a metal north;
but in the end, it is Donne's ghost who knows

Doom reads all maps. This cellar has no gongs
to clock my swans, although the air like a fog
is submarine with whispers, and her hair
trails like a bloom the suicide had kissed
some Hellespont ago, in waters sweet.
Her fingers like a coral hold her glass,
and here we swim, or float, like any dead
in a courteous ocean, in a formal mist.

But the music is no signal for tall gates
to open on Atlantis dreadfully.
It is a whisper tricky as a sin
to tickle the bottles, or to taint the mouth
with crooked singing. Gracefully I shall drown
down private ladders leading to clear wells
where mermaids prepare my capture. Let me clutch
one very last, before I lose my drouth

and negotiate my vintage for a smile.
There must be other ways to wear my wound

I think a moment. But her arms are soft.
Then let Love be an island, circled once
to peg a legend: Trite warriors of the flesh
said Love, like battle, and bowed in victory
before a goddess, tranquil as a dunce,
cold as the north, but tropic to their fee.

THE DOGE'S PALACE

Old worlds, and arias that clanged like toys,
all tender tinsel, monkeys, and out of date
poetry books, (the use and luck of Time)
these were somebody's furniture, not mine.
Reactionaries, princes knew my fate.
It was no lucky kingdom. It was mourning.

That day I walked the marble gardens, morning
was made public. The pages sneered at my food. Like toys
the ministers prinked in the squares, and named the date
a victory. Oh I was tired all the time,
and longed for my loss like a garlic, a fool's fate,
or a cool dungeon selfishly all mine.

And the general was the least friend of mine,
looked on me as the prime of necessary toys
for his game, and every single mourning
listed the casualties, and checked the date,
and read off the names, like a cook in time
for a broth. And his was the call of fate

to judge my son, and spill his tinkling fete
with a silver bullet. And they called it morning—
yanked me for a parade with flutes and toys,
girls with pink knees, and not a mother was mine
even if I had cared. The town marched in time,
and some fool bishop blessed the nasty date

with a dirty finger. But if I am out of date,
then so is his finger, his swishing, and the toys
he sprinkles the bumpkins with, and their morning
is as evil as empery. All fate
will overtake the people the same as mine,
will come in a republic at a time

till each public toilet proclaim election-time,
and horses vote their aliment, the date
studious with odors, scandals of health, and mourning
be their frog belching in the wind of fate.
But they have shaved me, shaken me, and mine
at last is the peace of a boy with his toys

in a rich corner — toys that are mangled, but mine.
That's no bronze wink of Time, their fire. The date
that they call morning, isn't: it's fake. It's Fate.

SONG

My enemy is looking for me
in the busy streets, standing on corners,
like an old man with a running nose,
mumbling and shuffling, muttering my name.

My enemy watches my window
from a cold doorway, smelling my dinner.
He bribes the mailman to read my news,
and he is grave and pensive at his game,

boarding the wrong train with a flat look,
following a man with a coat like mine,
sipping beer at my favorite bars.
Listen. This is the point I make:

a man falls from the eighteenth floor,
and nobody pushed him, the papers swear.
I have a notion of secret doors —
my enemy making another mistake.

EYE

A DOMESTIC NOTION
(*For Selma*)

Being a wife becomes you,
the way being an ocean
becomes the Venus of Botticelli,
who of such strength such
grace employed. And you, you

are the liveliest furniture here,
in that bed, this room.
You move with incredible logic
from dresser to chair, with
small, silk things at hand,

an occurrence of proven facts.
But vision's the least of facts.
We say, see a hill,
but it's not a hill.
It is the earth, no

self-respecting hill but would agree.
As when I watch you,
with an onion in your
hand by the kitchen-window, and
the thing becomes a sun.

THE EYE

Mite, baby spiders take the breeze,
and trail their lariats, sailing high seize
the first hook that locks at them, abode:
home has been sighted, lassoed fast.

Prisms of tight conspiracies
translate the text of plane on plane,
that seeing, and not sight, can key
and codify for lesson, sermon.

Target and dodger, whale and spider
appear, instinctive harmonies wrought,
sifted from moving lines, to rest
artistic as all algebra.

What mathematic hoists me up
with all my sums and all my suns?
If sight is witless, then witless hope,
and algebra is dice and dunce.

I am not looking as I look,
for stone-tricks and altar-trees.
The serious priest is slanderous,
but the spidery babe is all I see

who as the child of that great sun
can weave His metaphor so carefully
and wealthy-eyed. If all my wit
had half his flight, I'd sight my target.

River Full of Craft — 30 — Felix Stefanile

SPOILED BY ALL MY TYRANTS

Spoiled by all my tyrants, and whomped to bed,
But kissed for my blond curls from time to time,
then shoved to school as if I were the ewe
the principal has asked for, all my brothers
gruff and soon gone growing, to come back
and bring me all the grace of the Green Fair,
I had a precious training, and clean hands.
On the cold bench my mother creaked her grief
to understand my words: the school salute
I pressed upon the flag could only scare her.
O my dark kind, why have you left me bleating,
to learn trite courtesies and lowland ways,
when all I wanted was my rightful place
as the last son, beside my father's table?
Tell him that as I grow, my hair turns darker.

BROWN, ALL OF THE AUTUMN

Brown, all of the autumn, the manners of time
traditional, my mother walks to church
yielding the golden function, as she climbs
by sunny bannisters up to the porch

brass of the old God's office, as I wait
for nothing lovelier than a leaf like butterfly
to settle with yellow wing on the windy street
before my passage, till she catches my eye

and scolds me for my slowness. Pardon, God,
my absentmindedness across Your door,
and pardon death that comes so twinkle-toed
to this leaf on Your concrete floor.

IN THE SEA'S ALCHEMIES

In the sea's alchemies the visual sun
sinks like a whale, churning kinetic gold.
The veering gulls tear at my sight like a game,
and in the private poverty of my life
I hear for the first time the noise of myself.

You must fear the water to learn the Bible's navy:
how Noah swam the seven alcohols
freighting his God toward the trick of Ararat.
Thought of his tribe was the golden stunt of faith
to jimmy the salts of vengeance, the sea's walls.

Gold, gold will pip no legend with a style
until, like Noah, we fear the setting sun
gone down into the sea, o forty fortitudes!
and toward the final tides of our illusion
we must direct our emperies of drouth,

breathing a proper dread. Sailor, be like the fish.
Turn to that shelled mother of the world
who wore you like a wound once, slipped you in water.
The dry coasts are literate with towns,
but it rains in the neighborhoods of epiphany,

and sings us low a zodiac-spinning wind
his rainbow grammar and chance
naming gods, who wore no moral stitch,
but made the world. Sailor, say Land! like a flag.
But your guilt has gills. Your Noah was a fish.

TO WISH

To wish is farther than we thought:
a furthest off of tense
that credible as any nought,
can fool us only once,

when, vicious as all dreaming is
to futures of the will,
a present of severities
must satisfy us all,

and waning Will that features Won't
to leave us past surprise,
will learn that the dreaming head's a stunt—
a bubble with two eyes.

My wish was falcon to my fist
and father to my youth.
But if God lives, he's a stronger beast,
with feathers in his mouth.

CALM DAY

The sail I twanged like a guitar
now limply shrouds the lonely mast,
and where the buoys shone red, the shore
advances with a graying pull.
A management of bells invites
the soul to lose itself in mist,
and one lone feather, bobbing, writes
geographies of vanished gulls.

All's heavy, like a tired god,
healthy and tranquil to his sleep,
who planned his cot and scored his sod
like Saturn in the Roman wood.
The sky is easy as a sail
that shifts across a marble deep,
and in green seas an oak-tree whale
floats on the dark his heavy mood.

The lovers and their sailors watch
the colors of the evening flame,
and say a promise, each to each.
Children who ran all afternoon
watch now their windows blur with stars
that spin them in a lazy game.
The trolley, with a cricket's voice,
moves off in stealth beneath the moon.

Calm day, I count your gathering,
your summer colors running out.

Lazy and ardent locusts sang
playing out all the peaceful sun.
Now, tonic meadow scents have spread
over the offices of my doubt,
have promised me a dream I prayed,
and here's the moon to sleep upon.

ELEGY FOR MY FATHER

And when my father died I felt like Homer:
I shall remember him, slow as a turning god,
his face like a brown grape that sucked the sun,
his hands as real as Mondays.

And I shall remember my father, how his laughter
rapped like knuckles at the doors of my fears,
and all the walk of him at five o'clock
with the day's work like a round fist in his pocket.

And when my father died I felt like Homer,
imperative with melody and pride
to sing of all the trouble and gold of a hero,
that my hot words might shine with a bribe's powers

to buy his death with lucky metaphors.

VILLAGE ON MY BACK

Beneath the curve of hurried suns
in their hot rains' track,
I settled with my pain at once
like a village on my back.

My words I stung them out like tents
with banners, full of my news,
and my skin went around me like a fence,
and I walked with a squeak in my shoes.

Now as I grew, the land I say
I named my charming south:
my breath came merry, and full of oh!
but the winter pressed on my mouth —

and like a fish I dove from sight
beneath the eyes' lakes. Cleft
I was by a bump in the night.
Ah the blood's a river full of craft.

FEAST OF SAN GENNARO

And I remember figs strung on a wall,
and peppers, red and vicious, in a bowl
with thyme and fennel, on the window sill,
 beyond my reach, who wasn't very tall,

and sunlight spilling into the tiny room
to fall like plunder at my mother's feet
while at the table, calmly, calmly she beat
the dough as if it were a golden drum,

and father's silly knocking on the door
singing that Lola was his lady-love,
and chestnuts in my pockets, round and warm,
and Uncle Tony snoring by the stove,

and my fat cousins in their squeaky shoes
I can recall, and the quick, sudden pride
of father's laughter, and the wine, and how
tall yesterdays ago we never died.

COLOR AND LINE

Color on a sunless day: is it true color?
Street without tone, a shadowless gray,
the city's traffic in a concrete waltz,
horizons out, transparent, like the wind.

Perhaps the green is then most green,
the red not quite so naughty, and the yellow
yellow, arguing the scene.
In the apparent edens of the brain

do we need tropics on the sun
and vision's butterfly to tease the thought —
greens that leak with fruit, and the quartz-stone
sizzling, bonanza-veined, its tricky light?

The eye is a spurious camera. Behind
the watery eye a rudder clicks
its alphabet of triggers. See: how Ararat
was globed with colored fruits, but the doves

foreseen were white, and the lines black
upon the navigator's page, like news
printed to chart the fever of time, of time:
the deluge, lessons, colorless but right.

SCENES FOR A LIGHT OPERA

AN OLD REUNION

I went and marched to war,
but weather never promised me what for.
The shrill and braggart fife
did not remind me of my wife,
nor give me cause or caution for my life.
All friends were equal, out of pay,
and I awaited every day
for what I took to take me on the way.

Now, of a piece with the age,
it does no fever of my rage assuage
to think that years I fought,
to keep myself from adding up to nought,
were jolly jolly sixpence, nothing caught
out of my heedless nature's care,
that in distress with dress, my soul goes bare
to wear the same old war that I must ware.

I FOND ME A LOVER

(*To the memory of John Donne*)

I fond me a lover
in the boneblooming south:
a girl and a fever
to pucker my mouth,

a garland to yoke me,
the ease of her hair.
And nobody took me
before, before.

I caught a keeper,
o jailhood I wed!
and no pillow steeper
to bury my head.

A room to enclose me:
the shape of her lust,
fine fingers to choose me
and fondle me best—

and a lover to pace me
the miles of my blood
in weathers that please me.
In the dust gone red

she taught me such learning
who counted me won,
all in the slow turning
toward her breasts of stone.

FALL OF ADAM

From heaven my rainy father reigned
more Gabriel than the dawn,
walking how heavy in his top-dollar town
to wear the sun like a derby.

And what first knuckles were those alps
in such a calendar:
the oceans sang with forty throats
as he whistled in his splendor.

The animals elected him
their tipsy citizen
for his slow saunter and noise of grapes,
and a honey tammany.

To relish once that sudden rib's
omen singular,
he woke to all those monied hills
touching the round of her.

And from heaven my rainy father ran
with such a frightened girl,
inventing autumn as he went
than the night more Ismael.

SCENE FOR A LIGHT OPERA

I shall indulge you,
like a known spy
in a fat country.
You will be served.

My emotions are waiters cheating you gently.

I shall invite you —
Tourist at my bones,
dance for you with wooden smiles,
for the blonde coin of your face.

Like skis I bear you my love
from the histrionic alps,
and you may laugh at the churches
I wear on my vest.

But one quiet Sunday,
when the bells are on the other side of the air
and the roosters bragging,
I shall stick you with a silver knife,
leaving you under a slim, green tree
fringed with post-cards
like delicate sins.

After, we shall walk from each other,
toward those far countries of dishevelment:

but on your forehead
it will always be Lent Lent.

DAYS WHICH ENCHANT US

The afternoon
is a bronze bell
listing
in the uneasy days
blown from the hot mouth of Time.

Within me the blood lurches as to a tide.

The spirit eats locusts
in these deaths.
The light
is a poisoned honey,
and oh the inside fist to me
in a crazed season:

>orchards
>of foaming trees
>chanting
>their jazzy bibles overhead,
>apples
>like the breasts of Susannah.

I would have the sky snap open like a woman,
receiving this anger,
the terrorist light,
apocalypse of dogs, and scratching chickens,
and adolescents ravening by the sea.

As for the sun, that calm, ironic lion,

I would call his retreat,
I would blow his retreat
on an ivory trumpet—

Roland! crying
Roland!

MALESPINA

For Lucy

Nola and Palma,
towns like grapes in the sun,
snap in my thinking
with a quick, green sound,
mandolins
in a summer breeze —
but I haven't seen
either of these.

Maine I know,
and the claws of Cape Cod,
and in Virginia
hills like blood.
At Montauk I've run
from the breakers' flash,

but the Mediterranean
tastes of flesh,
and Pizzonuovo
sounds like a joke,
but there my father
first went to work:
eight years old
and driving his mule,
chewing his lunch
by a Roman wall.

Yes, Vermont,
I love you most,
and New York apples
are fine to roast,
and Long Island's the one
place to sail.

I'll take no town
built tight as a snail,
sick in the well
and dry as bone
just because I'm a father's son,
and him dead now
with a dream in his head
of Ottaiano:
raised eight times
from a volcano's
leaf and lime.

But it's the place
I've never been
that cries like a bell
the wars men win.

WINTER YEAR

Come to the general store, I cracked my barrel
against the bargain of a stingy grocer
who hauled my sack and sin from a hungry kitchen.
The gates of town closed fast, like an iron No Sir!
and down the snow flew, like the sky's own quarrel,
horizons of teeth that nipped my winter stitching.

I heard the geese go bong in my seven meadows,
and in the sky the moon flung, like a stone,
and the long road, my snake, with waking shuddered,
postured for traffics of ambush. Soon
the night pawed forth, and shutters slammed their rhyme,
and the crow ran hoarse, the cock stole time, stole time.

So moving, with my pennies, prophet, driven
by a tightrope hope to balance in perilous places
the fahrenheit I have to any haven,
I whistled my south in all the wind's addresses.
Snow jingled like new coins against my creases,
cold counterfeit to clink in the nearest tavern.

THE LEAVE-TAKING

I woke to a chill
and brittle dawn,
and all the April
frost-flowers shone.

I climbed a stair
to count my face:
the glass was clear
and let me pass.

Then from the hall
a shadow came,
and on the wall
wrote my name.

I watched the sun
come up the street,
like an old man
in an early hat,

and shut the door
from where I'd come,
while in my ear
clicked all my home.

And then I heard
the clocks of town
strike a silver word,
and I came down.

And I came down
through field and cove,
from that thin town
of taking leave,

with at my head
the dawn's quick chill,
though all the birds said
April, April,

and nothing stirred,
as I stood alone,
but Time I heard,
and I came down.

SPIAGGIA

That morning the sun led me down
to the pink beach beside the ocean
where boats played in the Hans Christian Andersen dawn,
beckoning my sophomore's devotion
to conch-shell myths, and the spill of mysteries
curved and wrought with the sea's histories,
and my island became a nation.

So I watched where the limestone cliffs
recalled me Matthew Arnold, but in an afternoon
full of yellow play and no seagull griefs
of nervous moment: brief shoring against the moon
that would come with its slow business among the rocks
translating into parables the shocks
of tide-wrack and wind-groan.

And then I heard the lobsters like Arabs singing
their bubble-tricky melodies, and the waltz-
ing of the weeds that moved with a shape of longing,
while frenetic buoys applauded all my faults
with iron hands, and the sky's private property
reared up blue fences shocking the trepass in me.
Then Time whitened like salt

under my toe, and locked like sun's tooth
at my shoulders, while easy and chilly —
as from a hiding place — the wind, like some youth
who knew me, neared, and I sucked in my belly

to watch a crab that shone like a heart in the sun
crawl toward me with pink fangs. And I started to run
crying Shelley Shelley Shelley

INSOMNIAC

Confer me pain my knighthood thoughts:
the clocks are strange; the house is still.
The rain's insistent tremolo
scratches my brain with many noughts.

It is a lively dark I sleep:
across the eyelids closing down
my pupils spell blood's velvet word
like the odd name of a foreign town.

And it's a tricky corpse I lie:
for easier than counting sheep,
the heart's blue minute is what I count,
the reel and twist of my history.

And where have all the princes gone?
I slowly wonder, as I feel,
while the spilled hours run like dye,
that my jig is up, my jinx is on.

THAT UNDERGROUND SUN

That underground sun that warms my feet
shines where Jacob's Ladder slants to the sea
and the cobblestones reveal me turtles brave.
I have come to a goodly meet-
ing among the rosemary the phlox and the peony.

That underground sun shoots forth a river of claws
in the meadow, with a whirlpool at my ears,
but slow the wind flows, and there are no flaws
in the big blue air where I am a swimmer
gracefully floating from year to year.

But I feel the claw and crab and funny cancer
pulling with tide-pull long from Venus to Maine,
and the sun burns at my flesh with the nip of a pincer.
Retrieve me, seas, where under the ground, sun reigns
and my bones' coral morrows will glow like a stain.

That underground sun gives me the lowtide blues
for a squirrel drowned in the spring, or white in the winter.
The sharks are flopping in the chimney-flues,
and the lake upstairs floats one long cloud
serene and still like a submarine hunter.

Oh Davey Jones is chirping in the arbor
and I shall have passage after his last swallows.
That underground sun is drowning in the tall waters,
and the tides are rip, and ripe the snails in the shallows,
and the King and Queen are wet, and their sons and daughters.

THE PATIENCE THAT BEFELL

10 Poems by Felix Stefanile

These poems are for Selma:

"Al cor gentil ripara sempre Amore"

Felix Stefanile

Some of these poems have appeared previously.

Acknowledgements are due:
POETRY: A MAGAZINE OF VERSE
SATURDAY REVIEW
ELIZABETH
HARPER'S
APPROACH
POETRY BROADSIDE
PRAIRE SCHOONER

© Felix Stefanile 1964
Printed in U.S.A.

GOOSETREE PRESS: P.O.Box 278, Lanham, MD 20801

The Butcher Boy

The day that I was born—despite my crying—
my father mopped the mess upon the floor;
my mother wept as though all hope went dying
in living, in the spite that urged her more;
the midwife was the only person trying,
for all of us, like a hero in a war.

The store was open, and the customers came
for meat, while I, like chop-meat in the back,
lay so much fat and flesh and born bone-lame;
my tears dried where they fell, in the sawdust-track.
My uncle called the future by my name
up front, and gave the customers their money back.

They crowded round to bless me with their coin,
old women in black shawls, and skinny ones
with hair like seaweed growing from the brain,
and toothless ones and fat ones, and a dunce
who danced to see me dangling from my chain
until the midwife clipped me, only once.

And, as I felt the death slip past my reach,
across the cobbles an old churchbell rang
and crabs in the sewers clacked, as on a beach.
I treaded air, a spider to go hang
thrusting in light, and when I found my speech,
my word and wail, the harpies round me sang.

You, Cowper, In Your Garden

You, Cowper, in your garden, where dozed,
or like a merchant mourning ruined seed
inscribed a sermon on a rotting Oak,
what simple news made you so comfortable?
Here, they are brave enough, my stiff-necked parks:
a cantankerous elm has burst its wired prison;
the privet, tough as plumbing, full of turns,
tugs at my sleeve with a persistent gesture.

The wind's horn rides bone fields down my bare sight
to where the El, like Stonehenge, flares at dawn:
no moral but the climb I have to make;
I show my age upon the rusty steps,
but that means blood of iron — I should know;
I grew where oak-trees have no strength to grow.

How I Changed My Name, Felice

In Italy a man's name, here a woman's,
transliterated so, I went to school
for seven years, and no one called me different.
The teachers hardly cared, and in the class
Italian boys who knew me said Felice,
although outside they called me feh-lee-tchay.

I might have lived, my noun so neutralized,
another seven years, except one day
I broke a window like nobody's girl,
and the old lady called a cop; his sass
was wonderful when all the neighbors smiled
and said that there was no boy named Felice.
And then it was it came to me, my shame,
and I stepped up, and told him, and he grinned.

My father paid a quarter for my sin,
called me inside to look up in a book
that Felix was American for me.
A Roman name, I read. And what he said
was that no Roman broke a widow's glass,
and fanned my little Neapolitan ass.

EGOTIST

The purest eye can pierce
no wall, by wit or wish.
Though paper-thin, the skin
is lock enough, is fierce
with matter-latticed flesh
that will not let you in.

Nerve-ends, barbed wires, cross
the ruddy trench of blood:
were Sin the sentinel,
still not a troop would pass
that bony platitude
I fret in, joy and jail.

Dear Stranger I must love,
in scribbled words, that code
will break, before I die
this Me we're guilty of,
what insight to invade
that hidden country, I?

HOMETOWN

The drunks sang hero to the moon, that like
a bill-collector, stalled along the streets,
wishing my old man home. A concrete lake,
the warehouse glittered under the wind-swayed lights
where a policeman stepped, head bowed, and whistling,
amazing the silence with his loneliness.
The dawn came grayly, with the gulls,
the slow ruckus of the milk-truck, and my mother
padding, a sheeted figure, to the door,
opening to a cold, tin-foil horizon.
The bottles she gathered rang like a white money
left by a clumsy fairy: in my dream
the church-clock clanged with a country tongue,
and sparrows clicked like pennies on the pavement,
saying the world was round again, like her.

My Long Lost Brother

               how he talks to me!
The snails upon their stems hide in their shells.
A raven spreads his velvet on the lawn
in the red evening, and how that little boy
so clumsy and so curly and so swift
tells his rainbow in my face! I wince,
watch stucco suck the honey from the sun,
and think that I will soon be forty-two.
How the light tinkles every move he makes,
my long lost brother! with his grace of grass.
His teeth are like white vowels in his mouth:
he says he is the King of Mushrooms now,
and that Black Gravel, Owl and the Bell
are waiting for me. At the bottom of the wind.
Here is a lesson that I cannot spank:
my little twin is sleeping on my dirt
and wants to know the cricket of my name.
He says the taste is what you would expect.

A Fig tree In America

They hang full jewel, clusters of ripe figs
on the soft vine, and stir like pregnant women,
bothered by a breeze toward new discomforts:
in a keen ache of fullness slowly stir.

August, month of Midas, touched gold
the green branch burgled by the birds and worms
where they hang, in serious attitudes, like bombs
in the heaving cockpit of my fierce remembrance:

my father, moving slowly through the ruins,
like Vergil in his baggy overalls,
to aim his spade as though it were a spear,
and kick, from a cold slum, the slags of Troy.

And here I stand, amid the brick and business,
over the ultimate exile of his grave,
to marvel at my mortal foreigner,
who struck a flag that still can fly so green.

A Poem For Selma

Water dripping: the insatiable voice
of the radio, sarcastic bee
buzzing through the cheap sunlight of our rooms:
the hall, dark as a warehouse, and our clothes
slumped over chairs, in silent, dreadful poses,
crumpled flags
slipped in a sudden ambush; piles of books
scattered, as slate torn in the morning wind
of our hurry-all, all our choice and chattel,
and we make for it, each night, from a long train
dumping us, like troops, to a dim outpost
in the domestic jungle of our lives.

That grouch, my shadow, waylays every move
she makes, for booby-traps galore
flickering under touch: the pillows staled;
papers, like clues, under the bed; cracked combs
her fingers cannot heal,
and the smell of a crazy kitchen,
where she burns to know the woman that she is.

Canned goods, in rhymes of color, stacked on shelves,
remember landscapes dreamed unleft
in the lucky midnight when our sleep was sound.
The clock, like rivers, flowed. The alley dripped
Babylon, and the rain fell —
moss on the wall, and mushrooms in the brick.

There is conspiracy in all these smells:
pine in the soap, and talcum in the bleach,
whore's air of roses in the insecticide,
all the expensive junk of cleanliness.
The ugliness of this poem is my love:
I think how even the germs are frightened by it.

Outside, a code of spectrums on the street
holy my prison with the prism's soul
I remember that morning waking, dizzily floating,
thrashing through swirling sheets toward reality's mud,
a paper-swimmer, tearing on the rocks of morning.

I tugged at the fur
of my long beast dream,
but the dog's nose was cold.

I staggered toward linoleum reefs
where my sun was, shining
in rich, aluminum stripes
on the radiator.

And then you woke, in that iron-colored air,
saying, it's time, not, as I ask,
is it time?
In the distance, over the rusty shacks of the morning,
that crooked map shaped in reliefs of gravel,
we heard a rooster crying impossibly,
and he was saying Peacock, Peacock, Peacock.

OLD MR. SKIRMISH

Montaigne, locked in his tower, read and wrote,
and made wry jokes to please himself, and lasted,
holding to his spirit by the throat.
Leopardi sang, while his health wasted.

And there was Byron, exile to the end,
as pretty as Cassandra though less pure;
died rich at last, his Bible near at hand,
almost a Satan pondering his cure.

Not powerful, nor rich, nor famous princes,
those metternich-mechanics of my fate,
obsess me: how we live and lose by inches,
always dying early, always born too late —

but pleader in his prison's bony room,
some lonely devil without home or haven
still scribbling operas about his doom,
like hell-bound Shelley. And mailing them to heaven.

For My Own Birthday

I asked Love for some time
to learn his lesson well:
passion was a crime,
but the patience that befell
sent me back to hell.

Then I told Enemy
to hurry with his hate;
he answered courteously,
Better even late —
wait, wait.

Now I'm moving north,
but there calls me south
the wind's song, coming forth
from both sides of his mouth;
I waste, I waste my youth.

A
Fig
Tree

in America

Felix Stefanile

The Elizabeth Press
New Rochelle, N.Y.

©1970 Felix Stefanile

Acknowledgements:

The poems collected here first appeared in the following publications: APPROACH, BELOIT POETRY JOURNAL, CHELSEAN EIGHT AMERICAN POETS (Villiers, London), ELIZABETH, EXPERIMENT, FINE ARTS CALENDAR, HAWK AND WHIPPOORWILL, HEARSE, THE HUMANIST, MIDWEST NEW MEXICO QUARTERLLY, NEW ORLEANS POETRY JOURNAL, THE NEW YORK TIMES, THE PATIENCE THAT BEFELL (Goosetree Press, Lanham, Md.), PERSPECTIVE, POETRY, POETRY BROADSIDE, POETRY CHAPBOOK, PRAIRIE SCHOONER, SAN FRANCISCO REVIEW, SATURDAY REVIEW, SPARROW, VOICES, WORD JOCK, and YANKEE.

These poems first appeared in POETRY: *On My Day Off, A Grouchy Poem; Services; A Late Elegy for a Baseball Player; An Old Bootblack in the Cafeteria; A Poem for Selma; Atlantis; A Fig Tree in America; Love Song and Song for Rory* (from *Some Songs for Billie Holiday); My Long Lost Brother; Brown; All of the Autumn; Sea Gulls; The Fortune Hunter; The Marionettes; Lullaby for a Dark Night; The Afternoon as an Aria; That Underground Sun;* and *Years.*

Old Mr. Skirmish first appeared in SATURDAY REVIEW,
© 1960 Saturday Review, Inc.,
reprinted by permission.

Grasshopper first appeared in PRAIRIE SCHOONER,
© 1957 University of Nebraska Press,
reprinted by permission.

Girl in the Garden first appeared in THE NEW YORK TIMES,
© 1962 The New York Times Company,
reprinted by permission.

This book is produced with the aid of funds
granted the publisher by the
National Endowment for the Arts

Manufactured in Great Britain

These poems are for Selma, my wife

CONTENTS

AGENT'S REPORT	81
ON MY DAY OFF A GROUCHY POEM	82
SERVICES	85
A LATE ELEGY FOR A BASEBALL PLAYER	86
HOW I CHANGED MY NAME, FELICE	87
AN OLD BOOTBLACK IN THE CAFETERIA	88
INVOCATION TO THE MUSE	89
A POEM FOR SELMA	90
YOU, COWPER, IN YOUR GARDEN	92
OLD MR. SKIRMISH	93
HOMETOWN	94
ATLANTIS	98
A FIG TREE IN AMERICA	100
SOME SONGS FOR BILLIE HOLIDAY	101
FEAST OF SAN GENNARO	103
MY LONG LOST BROTHER	104
GRASSHOPPER	105
AS I WENT OUT ONE MORNING	106
THE MAN WITH THE LATVIAN LOOK	108
SUNDAY MORNING	110
ANTONIO STEFANILE	112
THE REPORTERS	113
FOR MY DARK LADY	116
BROWN, ALL OF THE AUTUMN	117
SEA GULLS	118
AN INCIDENT IN FLUSHING BAY	119
MRS. CLOTHO, MRS. LACHESIS	121
HURRICANE	123
THE FORTUNE HUNTER	124
MALESPINA	125
A DOMESTIC NOTION	127
THE MARIONETTES	128
BELTING A SONG	130
THE GIRL IN THE GARDEN	132
THE BUTCHER BOY	133
LETTER FROM A FRIEND IN EXILE	134
STREET SCENE: THE DRUNK	136
AMERICAN D.P.	137
A LULLABY FOR A DARK NIGHT	138

AUBADE FOR PAQUETTE   139
THE AFTERNOON AS AN ARIA   142
CONVERSATION IN A STORM   143
BACK HOME IN INDIANA   144
ELEGY FOR YURI GAGARIN AND OTHERS 146
THAT UNDERGROUND SUN   150
SNOW BOUND   151
ELEGY FOR MY FATHER   153
A LITANY   154
YEARS   156

A Fig Tree in America

AGENT'S REPORT

I manage, like a spy, to check the country
of my past against our present treaties;
the weather that I carry is the same
I think, some weapons are outmoded—
That toy gun of a heart serves no more use
today than when I first shot off my load:
the aim is bad, and all my tubes are crooked.

I spill a little blood but get on still.
My fingers feel like they are touching mud
sometimes—a softness I had never known—
but my bones stay in place and every tooth
mere rage could want, through who knows what I want.

The landscape still repeats the old motif;
(the enemy has not relaxed its ways).
There is one moon, about as white as bread
and pocked with craters where my dream blew up.
The sun, like money, burns a hole in the sky
but the birds don't burn; the people ask for more.

The woods are a conspiracy. I think
the squirrel knows a joke he will not tell.
The fish refuse to sing, though in my dreams
I hear loud organ-tones of rocks and streams
where they convene, in submarine cathedrals.
Their castles are like bones, with ferns for drapes.

My hand still keeps the map, I read the lines;
they work a code to where the damage is
but every road, I swear, leads but to roam.
My God!, how lost I am! This war is mad;
nobody fights me, and I fight myself.

Each morning I rise from my mattress-grave
as shapely as a statue. I am clay
I tell you. Send my son. He can replace me.
He may know more; he has more vitamins.
I am a blood to ferry incidents;
if you know, tell me where to go from here.

ON MY DAY OFF, A GROUCHY POEM

On my day off the yards are full of women:
they chirp like sparrows as they flit about
and flutter in the wind in kerchiefs and scarves,
and pick through paths that bleach in the sun like laundry.
The business of their disarray amazes —

one in a house dress, nervous as a sparrow,
yanks at her brat, blond turnip, by his patch,
while another one in slacks and with big tits
handles and fondles her hair on a sunny terrace
with all the grace and ease of a snake-charmer.

Plucky and shrill they swirl, they slip about,
dragging at carts with dainty clumsiness
or clutching packages in their fine claws,
and I stand at my window, grouchy as a king
in a land of Menopause, where all Time bleeds.

Women! What have we done to you, to set you
here in this rubble of stores and parking lots,
with the cold smell of soap across your aprons,
the sour smell of children in your thoughts?
Do you remember Eden, loot and leaf,

the sun scattering beatitudes where they fell
in hurly-burly bullions of adolescence,
and do you remember weekends full of invention
when love forged Eve's name on a motel-ledger,
and the walls glowed in the twilight, and took fire?

A Fig Tree in America — 83 — Felix Stefanile

I must move away, and back to my poetry,
frills of papers and butts, and a memory
of Hansel and Gretel, Adam and Eve in the garden—
the wicked witch was only a mother-in-law;
and the butcher, padding his bill, is the only Satan.

SERVICES

On Sundays light, and a respect for Law,
prepared the time of day for our procession:
civically clean, the sunlight that we saw
shone through the stained glass like a God's obsession.

The stammering priest upon the podium
revealed the Word. To look the Light's reward
old women donned their glasses, and looked glum,
and yet the chalice glittered like a sword.

And I'd too much of wit that happy morning
to mind the dollar that my wife dropped in
the plate with the long handle without warning;
meanwhile the sun distracted, like a sin,

and the lean dust in a dry odor stirred;
the glowing pews an ancient polish breathed;
and girls, like small bouquets, spoke without words,
their brightness answering what the light bequeathed.

A LATE ELEGY FOR A BASEBALL PLAYER

He was all back,
his stance was clumsy,
ran like a horse,
smiled with a dimple,
but Time cut him,
as easy as that,

bowled him right over,
muscle and all, for
a crick in his honest back —
the wellwrought stallion,
cleats on his shoes,
and a hometown shoulder,

full of country bumps.
We read about Herakles
and the hairy Samson,
and fake Olympic games;
the whole world boos —
but here's Big Lou

whom Death bowled over
as the sun rose,
a lazy foul ball,
and a whole generation
of the running boys
pull up, cry loud

at what Death caught.

HOW I CHANGED MY NAME, FELICE

In Italy a man's name, here a woman's,
transliterated so I went to school
for seven years, and no one told me different.
The teachers hardly cared, and in the class
Italian boys who knew me said Felice,
although outside they called me feh-LEE-tchay.

I might have lived, my noun so neutralized,
another seven years, except one day
I broke a window like nobody's girl,
and the old lady called a cop, whose sass
was wonderful when all the neighbors smiled
and said that there was no boy named Felice.
And then it was it came on me, my shame.
and I stepped up, and told him, and he grinned.

My father paid a quarter for my sin,
called me inside to look up in a book
that Felix was American for me.
A Roman name, I read. And what he said
was that no Roman broke a widow's glass,
and fanned my little Neapolitan ass.

AN OLD BOOTBLACK IN THE CAFETERIA

I watch him stumble into the place,
dragging his speech behind him like a limp,
shuffling up to the counter next to me
to beg a coffee with the dimes of his eyes.

There is about him no humility:
his jigging muscles hold his chin alert
as if to face life's blows, an exiled king
from shoeshine country, dirty, but full of heart.

Placing a fist on the glass, he seems to sing
the news of his presence to an ignorant crowd,
waiting with a moan as plain as a hymn
for the boy with the Western accent to bring food.

And I catch the smiles they exchange, like prisoners
meeting in a dingy jail in a lean year:
a homesick boy, an old man crooked with age
carrying his coffee like a piece of fame

to where he sits beside the busy doors,
his strapped box set by him like a toy fort
stacked with the ammunition of his waste.
And as it passes, speaks to the World's shoes.

INVOCATION TO THE MUSE

I might as well say Love
a mermaid with green hair;
there's little love enough
in the sea down there,

and I'll break all the rules,
and sneak into your city,
and scrawl upon the walls
words to stir your pity,

and Critics calling halt
may ask me What's the use?
I'll answer, Mine the fault
and mine the muse.

A POEM FOR SELMA

Water dripping: the insatiable voice
of the radio, sarcastic bee
buzzing through the cheap sunlight of our rooms;
the hall, dark as a warehouse, and our clothes
slumped over chairs, in silent, dreadful poses,
crumpled flags
slipped in a sudden ambush; piles of books
scattered, as slate torn in the morning wind
of our hurry—all, all our choice and chattel,
and we make for it, each night, from the long train
dumping us, like troops, to a dim outpost
in the domestic jungle of our lives.

That grouch, my shadow, waylays every move
she makes, for booby-traps galore
flickering under touch: the pillows staled;
papers, like clues, under the bed; cracked combs
her fingers cannot heal,
and the smell of a crazy kitchen
where she burns to know the woman that she is.

Canned goods, in rhymes of color, stacked on shelves,
remember landscapes dreamed unleft
in the lucky midnight when our sleep was sound.
The clock, like rivers, flowed. The alley dripped
Babylon, and the rain fell—
moss on the wall, and mushrooms in the brick.

There is conspiracy in all these smells:
pine in the soap and talcum in the bleach,
whore's air of roses in the insecticide,
all the expensive junk of cleanliness.
The ugliness of this poem is my love:
I think how even the germs are frightened by it.

Outside, a code of spectrums on the street
holy my prison with the prism's soul.
I remember that morning waking, dizzily floating,
thrashing through swirling sheets toward reality's mud,
a paper-swimmer, tearing on the rocks of morning.

I tugged at the fur
of my long beast dream,
but the dog's nose was cold.

I staggered toward linoleum reefs
where my sun was, shining
in rich, aluminum stripes
on the radiator.

And then you woke, in that iron-colored air,
saying, It's time, not, as I ask,
Is it time?
In the distance, over the rusty shacks of the morning,
that crooked map shaped in reliefs of gravel,
we heard a rooster crying impossibly,
and he was saying Peacock, Peacock, Peacock.

YOU, COWPER, IN YOUR GARDEN

You, Cowper, in your garden, where you dozed,
or like a merchant mourning ruined seed
inscribed a sermon on a rotting Oak,
what simple news made you so comfortable?
Here, they are brave enough, my stiff-necked parks:
a cantankerous elm has burst its wired prison;
the privet, tough as plumbing, full of turns,
tugs at my sleeve with a persistent gesture.

The wind's horn rides bone fields down my bare sight
to where the El, like Stonehenge, flares at dawn—
no moral but the climb I have to make;
I show my age upon these rusty steps,
but that means blood of iron—I should know;
I grew where oak-trees have no strength to grow.

OLD MR. SKIRMISH

Montaigne, locked in his tower, read and wrote
and made wry jokes to please himself, and lasted,
holding to his spirit by the throat.
Leopardi sang, while his health wasted.

And there was Byron, exile to the end,
as pretty as Cassandra though less pure;
died rich at last, his bible near at hand,
almost a Satan pondering his cure.

Not powerful, nor rich, nor famous princes,
those metternich-mechanics of my fate
obsess me: how we live and lose by inches,
always dying early, always born too late —

but pleader in his prison's bony room,
some lonely devil without home or haven
still scribbling operas about his doom,
like hell-bound Shelley. And mailing them to heaven.

HOMETOWN

1. The drunks sang hero to the moon, that like
   a bill-collector, stalled along the streets
   wishing my old man home. A concrete lake,
   the warehouse glittered under the wind-swayed lights,
   where a policeman stepped, head bowed and whistling,
   amazing the silence with his loneliness.
   The dawn came grayly, with the gulls,
   the slow ruckus of the milk truck, and my mother
   padding, a sheeted figure, to the door,
   opening to a cold, tin-foil horizon.
   The bottles she gathered rang like a white money
   left by a clumsy fairy: in my dream
   the church-clock clanged with a country tongue,
   the sparrows clicked like pennies on the pavement,
   saying the world was round again, like her.

2. Eliodoro's neon
   LEO flickers at midnight from his crazy corner:
   Lion-whispering nickelodeon.
   Leo's legal, has a lawyer;
   every winter
   needs a warner.

   Money-sure
   of a public century
   Leo dared democracy
   and served us all —
   the Irish, the Negro neighbor,
   the pretty mulatto from the U.N.

One trip back, and one night home,
I tried the pizza just for old time's sake —
hot as ever, and the pepper
ground out of an "antiqued" shaker;
progress had come to the slums.
I missed the ignorant priests and grouchy nuns.

I thought of the public good
as a good man should:
Leo's public face
and the rat-tooth of his public grimace.
I thought of movie stars
playing tenement mothers, scrubbing clean floors.

When the nickelodeon roared
no saints came marching in.
I swirled toy circles in my gin
and thought of the heart's red eye —
nobody lives forever,
and somebody's going to die.

What housing project for the heart?
What suburb for the soul?
The boys were singing "Show the way to go home"
and I thought of Lorca in New York City
laughing for Whitman
and crying for Rome.

3. You can't go home again, said Thomas Wolfe,
who said a thing or two, but I still did:
the house has been torn down. An open grave,
the foundation showed its broken teeth.
The street I played in has another name;

where Bill was hit they put a traffic sign;
all the trees are rotten with the blight—
Chip and Meg and Tom have gone away.

As Pascal said, who said a thing or two,
you make your wager and win either way.
The new church looks just like a drive-in bank;
the stones no longer have CHRIST painted on them.
The Hill's been flattened down, and bulldozers
have filled the pond. Whatever was a Troy
that men should sing of her where no Troy stands?
Andromache moved to the Old Age Home.

As Papa said, who said a thing or two,
the day he signed the mortgage, the second mortgage:
the thing to do is chase the fury down.
He chased it and he chased it round and round;
when he ran out of breath he simply fell
and the lawyers wrapped him up in leatherette.
Now I get letters from the Old Age Home;
the weather's fine, and everybody's dying.

4. *Moon Over Broadway*

My moon is this full view of a brassiere
that glows from a cheap store-front rack in town:
like Marilyn a manikin looks down;
how beautifully her plastic turns a sneer.
Aegyptian eyes, mascaraed and severe,
bright as the jewels in her neon crown
blink past me, toward the silver and the stone
of the dead street by which I happened here.

I use her look, as any lost man would,
to count the Karnak-clutter praising her:
applause of awnings in the wind, the hum
of traffic snaking through the night, the stir
of shuttered, clacking stands where Worship stood,
and marvel — for such dark — what dawn will come.

ATLANTIS

That hunched and crowed town on the eastern coast
blinded the light of the moon with its own moonshine
and held the sea back with a cable line.
Lights Technicolor, rust, and rainbow almost,
when these winked out behind me, like a ghost
I toured the night, but I was never lost.

Beyond New Jersey then, I watched hills start
and toil toward mountains, like dark lava rolled
from Alleghany's brimstone red-and-gold
of sunrise, and my eastern heart took heart
to think that the stumbling sea had no such art
to follow where the mountains make a fort.

Then sliding down Ohio's punch-bowl, toward
the Indiana corn-fields, watched them wave;
my old prairie home made me feel brave.
And never guessed, till now, from what dark hoard
this landlocked moon that blinds me can afford
the light I lost, the sea I never heard.

Landlubber's luck, without a tide to race,
with money in my jeans, hole in my head,
I spy on strangers of squat, farmer's tread,
and wonder, for the years, how many seas
it took to sail their dream to this dry place.

That block of salt, the moon, is good and dead;
those meadows heaving in the summer rain

are not the sea I carry in my head.
I have a different kind of dream to bed,
and wrote this song, and saved my life again.

A FIG TREE IN AMERICA

They hang full jewel, clusters of ripe figs
on the soft vine, and stir like pregnant women
bothered by a breeze toward new discomforts:
in a keen ache of fullness slowly stir.

August, month of Midas, touches gold
the green branch burgled by the birds and worms
where they hang, in serious attitudes, like bombs
in the heaving cockpit of my fierce remembrance:

my father, moving slowly through the ruins,
like Vergil in his baggy overalls,
to aim his spade as though it were a spear,
and kick, from a cold slum, the slags of Troy.

And here I stand amid the brick and business,
over the ultimate exile of his grave,
to marvel at my mortal foreigner,
who struck a flag that still can fly so green.

SOME SONGS FOR BILLIE HOLIDAY

1. *Love Song*

   Mouse where my lover was,
   and scrambling down her chair,
   coffee boiling. Alley smells,
   and my soul, like sinus-trouble, begging for air.

   Crack in the wall
   and a wind like a worm in the crack,
   and the fried egg of the sun on my plate
   for the sun I lack.

   Now I think it over,
   the word I said was Wife.
   She is washing clothes in the cellar,
   thinking of her starched lover.

   O dance me on your clothesline
   to hang upon the wind,
   the ribbons out of Tuscany and Provence,
   and not my scarecrow sin.

2. *A Song for Rory*

   Think of Rory sleeping on the table
   and dreaming of his forty-seven windows,
   shoulders hunched, like jockey in the stable
   still riding gargoyle past the judges' windows.

A crazy wino crying soft and steady,
whose fingers prayed to rein his horse of lust,
while over the sprawled lumber of his body
the sun ran like a spider in the dust.

Remember how the Nickelodeon roared
like a wrong lion, and shook up his dream?
And he banged his head against his bed and board
until the very wind began to scream?

And for his bane's brawn, and his belly's fight,
cops offered mercy, lodgings for the night.

3. *Birthday Song*

I asked Love for some time
to learn his lesson well;
passion was a crime,
but the patience that befell
sent me back to hell.

Then I told Enemy
to hurry with his hate:
he answered courteously,
Better even late;
wait, wait.

Now I'm moving north
but there calls me south
the wind's song, coming forth
from sides of his mouth.
I waste, I waste my youth.

FEAST OF SAN GENNARO

And I remember figs strung on a wall,
and peppers, red and vicious, in a bowl
with thyme and fennel, on the window sill
beyond my reach, who wasn't very tall —

and sunlight spilling into the tiny room
to fall like plunder at my mother's feet
while at the table, calmly, calmly, she beat
the dough as if it were a golden drum —

and father's silly knocking at the door,
singing that Lola was his lady-love,
and chestnuts in my pockets, round and warm,
and Uncle Tony snoring by the stove —

and my fat cousins in their squeaky shoes
I can recall, and the quick, sudden pride
of my own laughter, and the wine, and how
tall yesterdays ago we never died.

MY LONG LOST BROTHER

                        how he talks to me!
The snails upon their stems hide in their shells.
A raven spreads his velvet on the lawn
in the red evening, and how that little boy
so clumsy and so curly and so swift
tells his rainbow in my face! I wince,
watch stucco suck the honey from the sun,
and think that I will soon be forty-two.
How the light tinkles, every move he makes,
my long lost brother! with his grace of grass.
His teeth are like white vowels in his mouth:
he says he is the King of Mushrooms now,
and that Black Gravel, Owl and the Bell
are waiting for me. At the bottom of the wind.
Here is a lesson that I cannot spank:
my little twin is sleeping on my dirt
and wants to know the cricket of my name.
He says the taste is what you would expect.

GRASSHOPPER

Gay jockey of the meadows, your cheap race
Revered from fear, and noted in the Bible:
All men remember seven years of grace;
Still more do they remember seven of trouble.
Such figures cannot measure your intent:
High as a Lilliputian kangaroo,
Over the leafy circus, witless went,
Prepared to do what Nature meant you to,
Poor Icabod! And leaned from your pogo-stick,
Eagerly eating up what the Old Testament
Regaled you with, and never got the colic.

AS I WENT OUT ONE MORNING

As I went out one morning
to take the pleasant air,
lolly too dum too dum lolly too dum day,

alephs and beths and
ghimels of lamentation
showered from the trees
and chirped on the iron fences,
and the Philip of me went strolling by
in search of his own lameness.

Up the avenue
and down the town, pink children
played at baseball and jacks and murder.
I laughed at an ugly woman;
from the rhetoric of her scorn
I limped to my repentance.

And as I went out one morning
to take the pleasant air,

just where I went strolling by
the shopwindows displayed John's head
lolly too dum day,
and a boy with the lungs of conscience
offered me false headlines
screaming Armistice towards Love,

and then, in the pleasant air,
all the mailmen hurried from me,
shielding their bags that never hold
news of emerald raffles in heaven;
only the same old bony town,
Christ on his twigs, Mephisto
to his Marguerite, and Lolly

too.

THE MAN with THE LATVIAN LOOK

is not going to heaven.
In fact, his destiny is negligible.
Like the anonymous porter,
he talks to corners of abandoned rooms.

He has no history
but unlike Liechenstein he is not lucky.

He is also confused:
when his watch says morning
he summons the moon, a girl with silver thighs.
When his watch says noon
he remembers evening fires in a village
as quaint as the town of Frankenstein
on Channel 13.
When his watch says night
he thinks of cows streaming across a road
like heavy children going to school
in a crazy sun.

Now he unfolds his lunch,
like notes to be sorted.
He gives me the smudgiest blond of a smile.
I ignore him. Avoid the sun-burn.
I decree him a heaven in the southern hemisphere,
along with the kiwi, on a barrier reef.
Consider these words my Balfour Declaration.

In the private park of my conscience
I'd come to sit and trim
the hedges of my soul,
and he cannot read the Signs;
he is walking on the grass.

SUNDAY MORNING

The leaky faucet chirps,
my private sparrow singing Sunday home;
the old clock hums.
And then nearer noises crowd around —
linen pets to snuggle to my wife:
pillows rustling, and the sheet's long smile
of sound, blinds rippling in the breeze.
Suddenly the walls fit into place;
lines follow ceiling, and the shadows break
like leaves that fall but make no fret. I wake,
and at the window watch for victory.
Sun comes over, watery, then bright,
rusting the roof-tops of the iron city.
Wires weave like rivers in the light;
iron turns to gold, in a backyard alchemy.

And in the alley, by his open door,
even the owner of the Delicatessen
casts off habits of trade, and sits on a milk-box,
shoulders hunched, and his hands clasped before him
in an old prayer of thought, and hearing no foot-fall.
Far off the church calls, with a clang of legend,
and the trees lean, like inefficient soldiers
in their poor plumes of green, against the houses.
Sparrows dart on the cobbles, and the pigeons,
as decorous as women going to service
with their own poise for parasol, stroll through sunlight,
gathering in small rainbows by the curbstone.

And yet, last night our sons lay down
and dreamed, not of their girls, but of ammunition.
I thought of all the world's impoverished millions
when smoke coiled in the slums, and the cluttered fences
clacked in the rain. All the dogs were howling.

Therefor, the Beaucoup Prince in his steady parlor,
watching the sun's calm vivas gladden the windows,
is thinking the sad thoughts of introspection,
lost childhood, and the Bible's anticlimax:

how ivy paled and withered on the trellis;
shadows deepened; as from a broken mirror
sunshine slivered, scattered into pieces
over the dirt and ash; from a dark window
someone bowed her head, her long hair flowing.

And also, I remember Augustine,
who feared this bold peace of the devil's weather
pleasing to the beasts of imagination—
Eden, shining, shining like a serpent,
Job amazed in his own meadowlands
to hear the birds clink in the trees like money:
the birds wished him good luck, and the birds lied.
O wish me well, poor sparrow, all the same.

ANTONIO STEFANILE

Nola, Italy: 1873-1959

You were a peaceful king, with many spies.
I think of all the slow and careful strangers
walking through the streets of foreign towns
with your horned, coral jinx tucked in their belts.
Now you are dead, the lurching continents
seem even less safe than they were before,
so scattered are we—like the Jews, surprised
to our identity this seventh year.
In Argentina children call your name:
who is there left now, old and queer enough
to write, and give advice, and pray for us?
New York and Canada send telegrams:
for where's the Elder now, of all our tribe,
the old man with a proverb and a pipe?
Your strength was foolish: therefore, luxury:
Anchises turned about, you carried us.
Beyond the sea's walls we remembered Troy,
and you, old shade, who stalked that abandoned rubble
like a good shepherd among sheep of stone.
In Boston an Irish priest trips on your name
to welcome to a world you had not walked
your late reality, your myth that bloomed
like mist beneath that moon of horoscope,
our banishment. O gentle, antique king,
of spirit large enough for large farewells,
the wind is but a roster of our names
that drop like seeds upon your flowering earth.

THE REPORTERS

perhaps an elegy

When the President was killed they invaded my sorrow.
Like the old Yankees,
full of equipment,
they broke all records:
the helicopters talked with the angels;
the Lions had lunch with the Lambs.
All the networks vied with each other
in the bright prairies of my grief.

What chromium weddings they promised us all
for Election Night—
faction function fiction.
Their machines,
as pretentious as Hammond organs,
measured the marriage of the North and the South;
East and West had a ball.

I heard instant-legends.
One of the reporters
sat on the marble floor, like a poet,
and traced with a cane the computer's zodiac—
like Merlin he pulled tricks and he was expectable,
and the statistics were true,
much more so than I was, or you,

or poor Grandma who thought he looked like Lawrence Welk.
By evening we were left our pretzels,

our crumpled newspapers;
the long tide of the night receded from the living-room floor;
we were marooned by facts.

Then the court-case:
scenting the loud miracle
the reporters trued the truth for the sake of history,
and you and me.
They insisted on the right of boudoir,
the right of *gabinetto,*
the right of spite.

I listened,
like a hypnotized neighbor —
behind curtains,
through the walls,
past fences and laundry,
while somebody murdered his wife.

Monotony enriched by so much strife
I marvelled and grieved for greatness:
the Queen was a tramp,
the Minister a crook.

Let's take a second like tomorrow
when the astronaut loses his hold,
and reporters will interrupt the news for the news,
even toothpaste and good cold beer
for the scoop of the year.

And they shall return, all through the night,
like impoverished gamblers in a Grade B movie,
their eyes hard,

their voices harsh,
their hands full of news like folding money,

and I shall keep awake, and you, and you,
and our tears will have absolutely nothing to do.

FOR MY DARK LADY

You are my headline: let men threaten war
and poison all the rivers of the air!
I know my own importance—it is you;
I do not fool myself with history.
And let them read the poor moon's frozen mind,
the idiots. I handle your slim bones
like instruments, and steer the galaxy,
a lucky fool who does not lack for fuel.

The earth revolves around me when you do:
then am I the ptolemaic mote to dare
Copernicus's might, proud of my dust—
his be the stars; you're my astrology,
where the Twins bound, and the Crab tears his house,
and my own astronaut, the Ram, runs on.

BROWN, ALL OF THE AUTUMN

Brown, all of the autumn, the manners of time
traditional, my mother walks to church
yielding the golden function, as she climbs
by sunny bannisters up to the porch

brass of the old God's office, as I wait
for nothing lovelier than a leaf like butterfly
to settle with yellow wing on the windy street
before my passage, till she catches my eye

and scolds me for my slowness. Pardon, God,
my absentmindedness across Your door,
and pardon death that comes so twinkle-toed
to this leaf on Your concrete floor.

SEA GULLS

How their bleak profiles grin and move,
eyes measuring the ground,
and uttering their madman's sound
as it for loss of love.

On wings as poor as tin
they counterfeit the luster of the sun,
flashing white, then golden
in mirroring ocean,

high, easy lords of Lack,
jackals of the sea
tracking the broken crab to tear his back,
with swift humility

scouring the junk Atlantis of the tides,
when mussels close themselves like fists,
and fishermen with worrying wrists
pull at their lines, and the coot hides.

The weather is no friend, they seem to cry,
but only happens, happens steadily.
They wheel and swoop. Beneath the sun
the bleaching harbor glows, like clean-picked bone.

AN INCIDENT IN FLUSHING BAY

The gypsy-orange of the garbage scows
streamed past my sight like silk in the wind
and gross light of that afternoon: a horseshoe crab
fluttered, in struggling spectrums, on the tide,
and sun and shade danced hard on the breakwater.
Those galleons of garbage tooted by,
safe pirates for my fond and hookey hoax;
I paddled after; New York burned to Troy
in a great, shining water thick as oil.

Like geysers the clouds spouted silently.
Past College Point, where the fog fakes and thins
to spray and sea-prink, I heard bully blasts
of old Atlantic's asthma, like the noise
of ice-bergs, and the fine terror of the gulls'
sheer coloratura off the island's coast.
Rocks roared dinosaur in the coming storm
and I was a sparrow, trapped in eagle's wind.

There my canoe undreamed itself: the raft
split like a biscuit just past Siri's pier
and splintered planks whirled in a zodiac
of dizzy water. With arms flailing out
I did a cart-wheel from the bottom up.
Past Cabot, Crusoe and Columbus then,
from war to wading, I made it to the shore.

All the town's compasses had turned to clocks;
nose leaking and shoes squeaking, I ran home.

My pants dried by the stove, limp semaphores
whose only signal was the seaweed stink
my father noticed. Mother, apron-sailed,
towed me past him; upstairs, she yanked my ear,
and then came back—she'd brought a glass of wine.
Their voices followed me, and trailed my sleep—
my father's high, not wanting to be fooled;
my mother's low, and trying to be firm.
Then there was silence; I was saved again.

And I dreamed a dream of the dolphin of the sea
on his warm and gravy wave, the brown-bread loaf;
ice-bergs of butter toiled alongside him.
And then I dreamed the crab with the club-foot,
hooded in iron for my horoscope,
the caesars of my month to his scissored kiss.
Like Venice-glass the old buoys sang my name,
voices whispering Come back! Come back!
And my old mother, bending over me
knew that I burned, and doused me with a tear,
saying, Wake up, wake up, it's just a dream,
and Pop went downstairs, where he blew his nose.

MRS. CLOTHO, MRS. LACHESIS

Across the street the two widows rake their lawns
and gossip, like gray robins, in the breeze.
The piled leaves are smouldering at the curb
and smell like cooking in the autumn air.
Behind them the grass ripples like chenille
with whitewashed stones for piping at the hem.
They are lonely. They are ageing. They are clean.
I find it in my heart to honor them.

Cold mornings, on my way to work, they stand
each at her kitchen-window dark with plants,
and stare past me the steps I have to go;
I turned around, but they have moved away.
I think about their houses, rich and void,
the man-smell of the wood that browns their rooms.
When I get home they're taking out the garbage —
white nurses to the duty of their dooms

the way they touch the bags so delicately
and set the lids down gently, without a bang.
I wish that they were cross or queer, or black
from shoes to shawl, like old Italian women,
to give my healthy pity a clear signal,
but no — they count their mail, or clip the hedge,
or toddling from the back with water pail
fill a bird-bath, wipe slime from a ledge.

Their chaste efficiency rules the whole world:
no rattling in the alleys, no doggy lawns,

no radios turned up on Sunday morning.
My wife makes sure to cover up the beer-cans
when we return from shopping, because of them,
and so does Mrs. Jones, and Mrs. Mears
who drives a car, and comes home pretty late
and cracked her garage-door this last New Year's.

I can mark time by either one of them,
for they have drilled the dolor from their dreams,
the summers hosing, every autumn raking,
each winter shaking salt upon the ice.
Sweet love of mine, sweet wife, if I go first,
I beg of you, please lose your wits awhile!
lean out the window, scream to be heard,
or kick up your heels and move away from town;
refuse those two, who are waiting for a Third.

HURRICANE

for Chester and Marjorie Eisinger

As from the Ark I view the perfect damage
rising like smoke form the sea:
buoy-bells bounding, their rust blacker than blood,
the whole dock clanking like junk moved about,
and stretching beyond my sight, attrition's wreck
of nasty slant—the whaledance of stove hulls.
The anger in the sky is quite strategic,
hitting the beachfronts with a skillful lash;
awnings sag like flags that dip in war.
My mind turns to that Mayor of all evil
the cop himself, in his wide rubber hood,
guiding our traffic through a sea of stone.
The future breaks behind us with a peal
of thunder loud as rubble being dumped;
old neighbor Never-Ready lurches past
as drunk as a Titan from his cloudy walk:
his mess repeats the message of all mud
in this old-fashioned forty days' weather of bombs
and my mind staggers for all picnics raided,
sign-posts torn down, chickens strutting in terror,
dogs howling, windows darkening in the soot
of sudden night, and the walls shining like bones,
arthritic ghosts of forms, shackles, frames.
Rain, that old chase of conscience, is forcing us
with rat-a-tat-tat as clear as a machine-gun
back to our caves and tunnels, our dry fort,
somewhere sure center, wrung by attitude:
there is a leak in time, and the day bleeds.

THE FORTUNE HUNTER

There are four dangers
the gypsy said:
> a man with a beard,
> a lady with a lavalier
> and a dog with the pox.

And what of the fourth, I asked her,
but there she was:
a plaster statue in her coffin-box.
Is and was and might-have-been,
I put another nickel in.

There are three loves
the gypsy said:
> a girl with a long look
> and a girl with a laugh.

And what of the third, I asked her,
but there she was:
smiling her fake smile, a photograph.
Is and was and might-have-been,
I put another nickel in.

There are two paths
the gypsy said:
> and one leads down to the coast.

And what of the other, I asked her,
but there she was:
my mummy Queen, with all the aces lost.
Is and was and might-have-been,
I put another nickel in.
Stranger, call my kith and kin.

MALESPINA

Nola and Palma,
towns like grapes in the sun,
snap in my thinking
with a quick, green sound,
mandolins
in a summer breeze —
but I haven't seen
either of these.

Maine I know,
and the claws of Cape Cod,
and in Virginia
hills like blood.
At Montauk I've run
from the breakers' flash,

but the Mediterranean
tastes like flesh,
and Pizzonuovo
sounds like a joke,
but there my father
first went to work:
eight years old
and driving his mule,
chewing his lunch
by a Roman wall.

Yes, Vermont
I love you most,

and New York apples
are fine to roast,
and Long Island's the one
place to sail.

I'll take no town
built tight as a snail,
sick in the well
and dry as a bone
just because I'm a father's son
and him dead now
with a dream in his head
of Ottaiano:
raised eight times
from a volcano's
leaf and lime.

But it's the place
I've never been
that cries like a bell
the wars men win.

A DOMESTIC NOTION

for Selma

Being a wife becomes you,
the way being an ocean
becomes the Venus of Botticelli,
who of such strength such
grace employed. And you, you

are the liveliest furniture here,
in that bed, this room.
You move with incredible logic
from dresser to chair, with
small, silk things at hand,

an occurrence of proven facts.
But vision's the least of facts.
We say, see a hill,
but it's not a hill.
It is the earth, no

self-respecting hill but would agree.
As when I watch you,
with an onion in your
hand by the kitchen-window, and
the thing becomes a sun.

THE MARIONETTES

See how they dream their wooden dreams:
oak legends are in their painted eyes.
Their ardor is of crepe and chalk.
The fire is their only surprise.

Catch how they mouth their gargoyle talk;
they even love with a scratching sound.
The fire is their only surprise,
Pinocchio burning himself to the ground.

Watch how they dance their clacking dance;
their kiss is like the breaking of a box.
They would sprout leaves like fingers of sense —
Master Gepetto, how they dance,

sauntering past with chirping knees
through the proscenium's feast of eyes,
wanting not to be made of wood.
The fire is their only surprise.

City of iron metaphors,
the children applaud their angular pranks
as their freak noses bump in fiction.
Do they hope that mothers will offer thanks?

See how they turn their necks of bark,
wound and wired for noise and friction.
They are not muddy children lost in the dark.
The fire is their only surprise.

Friend Cricket, your ardent piccolo
weeps from the wall like a prophecy.
They are so lonely racked upon the shelves.
They can weep splinters if only they try.

They're not content to be their wooden selves,
plotting a vegetable jacquerie
with their sinister sonorous Italian names
dreaming some varnished mythology.

Friend Cricket, you bug-christ on the wall,
Pinocchio, brother to the Cross,
murdered you twice, with hammer and stick.
They are all cousins to Joan's stake.

The fire is their only surprise.
They love a green and yellow courtesan
with a silver dress and amber eyes.
The moon is their favorite citizen.

And all unsteadied by their pilgrimage
to this lost season, like a sleeping town
visited by their pushcart prompt parades
I spy a hundred wooden strangers in the lemon dawn

shouting I love you in their fey dialects,
their chatterbox tarantellas waking the glades:
Columbina, the barking of Melampo,
the toy apples of Giuseppina's breasts,

coming back from the ultimate thules of illusion,
and Puncinello, staring with eyes of pearl,
singing I love the child with the blue hair,
I love the green and yellow girl.

A Fig Tree in America — 129 — Felix Stefanile

BELTING A SONG

They are writing
skinny poems
nowadays; the
trick is to hone
the rhetoric down
as with a knife,
a keen logic:
short words, short truths,
like True and False,
the syllables.

The heart has hips.
The skinny boys
see only its
cartoon arrow-
like tip, as in
Sweet Valentines.

Good and evil
I leave to liars.
I stick to what's
sacred and sinful,
a heavier thing
that takes longer
and isn't cute.

And how do you
carry that tune,
the whole burden,

unless you've got
meat on your bones
asked Caruso?

H o w   a b o u t   t h a t ?

THE GIRL IN THE GARDEN

inscription for a Cook-Book

It is a garden: in the morning light
the path glows smooth as pewter where she stands
with gathered fruit like baubles in her hands,
all streaked and silvered from the dews of night.
On the lost branch a sparrow, full of fight,
accuses her and her bright contrabands;
I dream my dream of calm and quiet lands
where every bird and girl is just as bright—

where the wide table, like a banner spread,
the morning's blazon shows: heraldic grain
the lover and beloved share as one;
where bold as bullion glows the golden bread,
and, lost in thought and grateful for my gain,
I watch birds fly my letters to the sun.

THE BUTCHER BOY

Oie mamma! piesce fritt'e baccalà....

The day that I was born—despite my crying—
my father mopped the mess upon the floor;
my mother wept as though all hope went dying
in living, in the spite that urged her more;
the midwife was the only person trying,
for all of us, like a hero in a war.

The store was open, and the customers came
for meat, while I, like chop-meat in the back,
lay so much fat and flesh and born bone-lame;
my tears dried where they fell, in the sawdust-track.
My uncle called the future by my name
up front, and gave the customers their money back.

They crowded round to bless me with their coin,
old women in black shawls, and skinny ones
with hair like seaweed growing from the brain,
and toothless ones and fat ones, and a dunce
who danced to see me dangling from my chain
until the midwife clipped me, only once.

And, while I felt the death slip past my reach,
across the cobbles an old churchbell rang
and crabs in the sewers clacked, as on a beach.
I treaded air, a spider to go hang
thrusting in light, and when I found my speech,
my word and wail, the harpies round me sang.

LETTER FROM A FRIEND IN EXILE

. . . I move among them, neither spy nor slave,
though like a spy I hoard my poverty
and like a slave I count their property
as something strange, and good, and not my own —
for what I touch here, brick, or bark, or bone,
does not touch back the way my fingers felt
the gritty answer of my crumbling hearth
the day I threw my name upon the fire
and ran my nail across the mantel's crack;
(it wandered, like a river on a map).

But the map's gone, and my lost country gone,
names of cities changed, our temples toppled.
Our children have been herded into pens,
our strong men run away to rocks and caves,
our women tossed like baggage on the shields
of the barbarian. And I am here, in exile,
ghost of a guest to all the gentle hosts.

Ingratitude? No. Thanks are in my heart:
I thank these men for the sound their footsteps make
in the safe night, for their moon's long-legged strut,
their silver Daddy puffing on his pipe
in fifty miles of corn. I thank the dawn
for happening in the sure way it does,
like a fine woman, with her apron gathered,
draping the light's clean clothes on all the lines.
I thank them when I close the door on them,
and hear their voices laughing down the hall,

then fading, as though voices became birds,
and fussed upon the branches, and grew still.
Like eager mutes, the shadows talk to me,
and in the darkness all my shades agree.

But what man needs a friend who will not grieve
when it is time for him to grieve, a friend
who puts his was too soon away from him?
If home is where the heart is, as you say,
then I still burn for my own broken hearth.
You must forgive this, as the sun forgives
the balked raid of the night on your bright fields.

STREET SCENE: THE DRUNK

Four corners watching him,
he stumbles into the street, into the traffic,
patiently shuffling, like a gladiator
bloodshot and rumpled, in a loud arena.

Whinnying wail of wheels, and motorists
flailing his fear,
he bellows back, his cry
scattering imagination:

while a terror-stricken woman,
screaming and honking,
grinds to a stop before him, almost fainting.

Then a dozen horns blow organ-tones
to form the anthem he will march to,
making the curb at last, alone, alive,
to stand in sunlight, dripping miracles.

And the barber, still holding his scissors
runs back to his shop;
the news-stand owner, thrilling to prospects
of cheap destruction, turns once more to his pennies,

and where the old drunk walks the crowd makes room:
a shaggy aisle he struts through, like a King
whose country is **Plague.**

AMERICAN D. P.

I left four rooms, of stucco and of brick,
my landlord dong his arithmetic,
a street as noisy as a Moslem square
in a spy movie — but my girl was there.

I left the broken beach-chair on the porch,
and in the bathroom half a pound of starch,
and in the kitchen-sink the coffee cup
that I'd been holding when the truck pulled up.

I left my mother, getting on in years,
and two good buddies who owe me for beers,
and thirteen sparrows sitting on a fence,
and one bill still unpaid, of forty cents.

Now, in the center of the continent,
I want to know where the oceans went.
As for these sycamores, what's the feat?
Back home our trees can push up through concrete.

I travelled for three days and half my life
with a torn map, some books, and a pale wife,
to beg, a pilgrim, at some stranger's door
the right directions to grocery store.

LULLABY FOR A DARK NIGHT

Leopardi sleeps in peace
underneath the cypress trees;
Andrew Marvell's also done
with his hurries in the sun.
On this night that shadows fall
like leaves blown against a wall,
Conscience plays at counting sheep:
soul, o soul, I cannot sleep.

The dog howling up the road
doesn't do me any good,
and the moonlight, pale as bone,
shines on everything I own.
While the bones that in me burn
shiver for the song they spurn,
Conscience plays at counting sheep:
soul, o soul, I cannot sleep.

And one sleep I cannot fake
lies inside me wide awake,
like a miser at his board
adding up the years I've stored.
When I close my eyes to test
whether he is laid to rest,
Conscience plays at counting sheep:
soul, o soul, I dare not sleep.

AUBADE FOR PAQUETTE

in memoriam Guillaume Apollinaire, d. 11/13/18

It is a sincere Spring

The birds are shitting in the trees

I think of words you can't put music to

I wanted my poems printed in the Bible
But the joke's on me
Here everybody speaks English
They are going to bring me up to date

The Horoscope Party failed to win half percent of the vote
I shall be off the ballot next year
The dwindled gold of a false religion impoverishes me
Even John XXIII might have disapproved good father
The windows predict weather
I am alone hoarding my aorta
Me and my uncanny dignity
All debts paid

Come my Paquette
Let us imitate Mars and Venus
Let us devise couches
Let us invent struggles
Let us obey the moon and the nine butterflies of the sky
Let us race around each other
Like Ptolemy let us refuse Copernicus

My allusions weigh me down for the code inside me
This gift of tongues this Aesop's Feast of betrayal
Anything to prove myself wrong in the face of smuggery
The seven clerks of the week

I was born on the number 13
I have been a race-horse ever since

I have a big mouth and I babble in the wrong places
My charm has brought me small profit
Even with a moustache and wavy hair
Delusionary maidens have plotted I have obeyed
Ah wife what hurricanes of regret
I am a lost bet
Money little enough
Down the avenue of ambition
Down the avenue of obsolescence
And all my glands sporting

Come my traitor
Lie to me
I dream of my youth as the Flying Dutchman of legend
There are fogs in my head

Come my traitor
Obsession of memory
The spring is here
From the barracks of the sun
Troop the yellow soldiers
Each bearing a rifle made of honey

Let us jeer Progress
The football hero

Cleated Hercules and vain Achilles
All that efficient misdemeanor

Our land is a parking-lot
Ruins and slogans and end-zones
I marvel that the unmiraculous birds
Have homed it back to the garbage
Only the incurable Negro cast his shadow
Over the Coney Island Sea
Mirages true my fake
And show me Whitman's face
The sparrow with the tricky mouth
Says his four-letter word

Come my traitor
It is Spring
Aries the horned god
On such a day it is good to sweat
There no guitars for this ailment
No sweets for this tune

My villages are rubble
Because of your glance
This poem is my self-defense
This parachute of concrete

THE AFTERNOON AS AN ARIA

The afternoon was an aria from Verdi;
the strolling cop beat time with casual club,
and the statues, courteous in stone,
dreamed in the humming shadows of the park.

The breeze was a nickelodeon of pigeons
and I called to my girl by the railing
come my lovely, away from those stone benches,
and dream with me of a prefab in the sky —

a duplex with green shutters, and furnished with squirrels,
and you, my little wife, in a silver kitchen
frying me bacon and gold,
while I, with a brand-new pipe, stand by the varnished mailbox,
gently murdering salesmen on the lawn.

CONVERSATION IN A STORM

in memoriam Professor Bird Stair, 1881-1958

We sit and talk. We sip our steaming rum
   and the wind blows.
Almost I wish I'd never come
     too much of weather's here,
    as the wind drums its long parade of snows
     down the black air.

Your books surround us, and their shining stacks
   answer the light
we try to make, who've turned our backs
    upon the surly blast,
    and the old wuthering at the window, Night,
     scaring us fast.

The room rocks in the swirl, and the drapes flail,
   shiver in the wind;
our words, like birds, fly low in the gale—
    a shrill and earthbound pride—
    meanwhile the moon has blown and thinned,
     and the stars slide.

Such science as man manages for Storm's
   ferocity
can warn, but your hearth-fire warms
    as Science never knows:
   you poke a flame; a hole in history
    sputters, then glows.

BACK HOME IN INDIANA

I get home,
like Charlie Chaplin,
all my dirigibles floating.

Gimpy from work
I sit, and drink, and think
there is much sailing to be done in Indiana —
at least one good ocean to dig,
some seventy thousand sea-gulls to be imported
and the right kind of foreigner, the wrong kind,
with black hair, gold teeth and a lucky parrot.

Across the Wabash one day
I'd heard Mexican field-hands, their delicate noise:
real Indians in Tippecanoe County,
right next to the Methodist Church.

Montauk! Montauk!
I cried, in my mind's leap,
thinking of the last page
in *The Great Gatsby* —
the homeless shore,
naked unnamed,
the dunes of Long Island swirled like carpets
ready for the tread of Europe.

And here, in the central plains, the final result:
history, a cleared table;

corn, heaped up like bullion, like the cross-over vote.
Safe from the pull of the tide and the smell of the moon
there is no rocking the boat in Indiana.

ELEGY FOR YURI GAGARIN AND OTHERS

Dear Gagarin,
family man and enemy.
I send you regards from Grissom, Chaffee and White
who cannot speak for themselves
as I can,
though I do not fly,
and from my wife
who is afraid of electricity.

    Your fame
I had sense not to envy;
as for our mistress the moon
I was jealous enough:
That white motel,
my imagination tilted
like a pinball machine
and you locked in it,
good citizen,
honest pinball.

I also send regards
from the good soldier Schweik
from Huckleberry Finn
who was luckier than any of us,
from Kilroy,
from Bill Mauldin whom I have not even asked,
from Montezuma
who never had his coming to him,
from Don Quixote—as tattered as a flag —

from that liar Galileo,
and from my mother who blames the weather on the atom
                                                    bomb.

I see you
approaching groceries
like any voter,
tongue in cheek,
hand on bill-fold
and an eye on the little cashier's behind.
I do not see you as a hero,
I who am such a clerk of a man,
reciting history,
counting the casualties every Sabbath,
but Troy is always losing the war and yet we sing of her;
what quarries our ruins make!

I see you as a man who snores,
with hair in your ears,
a regular appetite
and no reason to hide it.

You charmed us
like a pool-player:
you kept your mouth shut
and your eye on the ball.
Your modesty protected us more than you.
I imagine you embarrassed,
your wife blushing,
your neighbors smirking with that clear smirk
all neighbors entertain
when a good thing happens right on the corner
and they cannot be blamed for it,
and the mailman wanders about, saying he knew you.

I do not romanticize Russia
which ends in an 'a' like America;
I am a Little Italy of a man
and full of tricks.

What can I say you have not heard?
Glory belongs to the Mass.
Perhaps you will not hear my Alleluia,
but there are deaths it is proper to grieve
even in another country.
My irony is my own form of grief;
some people squint to see better.

I give you a wrong poem,
conscious of the sacrifice.
I mourn you in such terms
as the Milky Way will make room for:
tonight it is dressed like an altar;
Orion shines like a priest.

In my dreams I shall look for you
at the parking-lot, our only airport
in this small town.
The machines tinkle,
in the breeze the skirts of the girls go up,
the signs say Hamburger.
The invitation is genuine and the money is real.
When it is dark
the letters will glow
and I shall spell Yuri, Felix, and Anonymous.
What a loyal night to be sad in.

Dear Yuri,
so many kings have adored you
it's time an unimportant poet
awarded you an inexpensive poem.
We do what we can.
This takes pride.

THAT UNDERGROUND SUN

That underground sun that warms my feet
shines where Jacob's Ladder slants to the sea
and the cobblestones reveal me turtles brave.
I have come to a goodly meet-
ing among the rosemary the phlox and the peony.

That underground sun shoots forth a river of claws
in the meadow, with a whirlpool at my ears,
but slow the wind flows, and there are no flaws
in the big blue air where I am a swimmer
gracefully floating from year to year.

But I feel the claw and crab and funny cancer
pulling with tide-pull long from Venus to Maine,
and the sun burns at my neck with the nip of a pincer.
Retrieve me, seas, where under the ground, sun reigns
and my bones' coral morrows will glow like a stain.

That underground sun gives me the lowtide blues
for a squirrel drowned in the spring, or white in the winter.
The sharks are flopping in the chimney-flues,
and the lake upstairs floats one long cloud
serene and still as a submarine hunter.

Oh Davey Jones is chirping in the arbor
and I shall have passage after his last swallows.
That underground sun is drowning in the tall waters,
and the tides are rip, and ripe the snails in the shallows,
and the King and Queen are wet, and their sons and daughters.

SNOW BOUND

for Harold and Helen Watts

The vine, whose Persian splendor draped the house,
has withered; by the winter all its veins
had tightened, shorn of leaves, to knotted chains
that in the distance, in the wind's carouse,
seemed a web flailing. Now, for man and mouse
all meaning's equal — snow, freezing rains.
The fire may free us from our aches and pains,
but the solstice, like a spider, stalks the house.

The sun blinked out a signal, then went weak,
commanding notice but no message clear.
The geese struck in the hoarse voice of the year;
their clatter dwindled to a distant creak.
Whatever the wind says, it doesn't speak
my language: as one homesick, all I hear
is the lost slang of leaves where no leaves are,
and the storm scatters runes to read my wreck.

I dream of horsemen on the roof that ride
my seven sins, like bandits in black cloaks;
my small rooms shift like pebbles in a box
and the wind's at the door, with crazy stride
tearing all around to try the locks.
Thin shapes show at my windows, white as pox,
and start me thinking of a place to hide.

I cannot tell myself, in this distress,
anarchic matter's working the vast span

now murdering me from Southampton to Spain
and scratching the Atlantic's frozen face;
this midnight of the year, Copernicus
himself might think that he was Ptolemy's man,
and I am thinking as hard as I can
that we are targets, more's the worse for us.

My floor-boards squeak. The cold mouse underfoot
goes whistling in the dark the same as I,
while overhead the stars, stalled in the sky,
grind their slow wheels along the thickening route
of sleet and snow. The daylight falls like soot,
and the zodiac zeroes in, its radii
a dozen cannon ranged around the high-
hung earth, poor pot-shot kite that clanks about.
I'd better hope. The devil with my doubt.

ELEGY FOR MY FATHER

And when my father died I felt like Homer:
I shall remember him, slow as a turning god,
his face like a brown grape that sucked the sun,
his hands as real as Mondays.

And I shall remember my father, how his laughter
rapped like knuckles on the doors of my fears,
and all the walk of him at five o'clock
with the day's work like a round fist in his pocket.

And when my father died I felt like Homer,
imperataive with melody and pride
to sing of all the trouble and gold of a hero,
that my hot words might shine with a bribe's power

to buy his death with lucky metaphors.

A LITANY

It is a lovely day:
the river weeps;
like the cardinals of the Pope
birds share their disagreement,
and some red skelton of a squirrel
razzes the whole population.
A scarecrow imitates the pride of the wind —
he is the only mother the brown mouse has.

It is a lovely day:
the river weeps.
Next door my neighbor
cut his hand on the mower;
for him the grass bleeds and the smell is good.

Later,
worms will come,
wearing rainbow horns,
but the danger is fake.
They are protected as scapegoats
by slovenly taste
and the look of technicolor. Birds avoid them
but not Jean Henri Fabre. The river weeps.

How shall I say the day is good?
Across the street
Pain had a baby:
I wish that I could name her Algebra.

The river tastes like beer,
all camouflages work —

flesh of orange bone of salt
sex of cannon and the candy of sentiment,
shapes of sheep in stones on sunny hills.

The postman resembles God
on a lonely street; the grackle
wears a locust for bowtie on his purple vest;
the river weeps.
My coffee tastes like spit without a name.
It is a lovely day;
you must believe me.

YEARS

I am dwindled to a small country,
hauling my body
over queer ledges,
like Pinocchio,
to talk a tiger off the road.

Words do not happen as they should anymore,
even on beautiful days
when the weather wears my skin:
I see what I cannot say —
a cop in the park, whistling;
the moon, drifting past my window
like the smoke of ruined nations.

Or songs that I dream, like
    Mother Damage, Mother Damage
    the sea is always winning,
    the fish is at his window
    and your belly the color of sand.

Here now's the slum of myself:
a few lines,
a pot belly,
books in my room
scattered like birds
caught in a strong wind
and I never heard it at all.
Staring at my mind.

When the sun sets
I shall light a candle,
and tell it to burn.

FELIX STEFANILE

EAST RIVER NOCTURNE

The Elizabeth Press
NEW ROCHELLE, N. Y.

ACKNOWLEDGMENTS

Some of these poems first appeared in the following publications:

AESOP'S FEAST, COASTLINES, ELIZABETH, ITALIAN AMERICANA, KAYAK, THE NEW YORK TIMES, PERSPECTIVE, POETRY, POETRY NOW, QUICKSILVER, A SUIT OF FOUR, VIRGINIA QUARTERLY REVIEW, & YANKEE.

A CARTOON FOR ARISTOTLE appeared in POETRY.

IN THAT FAR COUNTRY appeared in THE NEW YORK TIMES, © 1959 by The New York Times Company. Reprinted by permission.

ON THE VANITY OF HUMAN WISHES appeared in a SUIT OF FOUR, Purdue University Studies, © 1973 by the Purdue Research Foundation.

FUISSE by Andrea Zanzotto, reprinted from POESIA ITALIANA CONTENPORANEA (1909-1959), ed. G. Spagnoletti, no date, Guanda.

© 1976 Felix Stefanile • PRINTED IN ITALY

These poems are for Selma.

EAST RIVER NOCTURNE,

notes for an Epic

Bilbea, I was in Babylon on Saturday night.
I saw nothing of you anywhere.
I was at the old place and the other girls were there,
                              but no Bilbea.

Carl Sandburg

MIST *I don't believe the sleepers in this house*
Know where they are.

SMOKE *They've been here long enough*
To push the woods back from around the house
And part them in the middle with a path.

MIST *And still I doubt if they know where they are.*
And I begin to fear they never will.
All they maintain the path for is the comfort
Of visiting with the equally bewildered.
Nearer I plight their neighbors are than distance.

Robert Frost

CONTENTS

THE LOSER'S CLUB	167
PROEM	169
THE DAY WE DANCED THE SAINT	171
EXILES	173
SLUM	176
ULYSSES ARRIVES	177
EAST RIVER NOCTURNE	178
HOMETOWN	184
MUSE: TO WRITE IT DOWN	186
THE WEATHER DIDN'T DO US ANY GOOD	188
AMERICAN LEGEND	190
A CARTOON FOR ARISTOTLE	193
POEM IN THE MANNER OF WALLACE STEVENS	194
IN THAT FAR COUNTRY	195
ON THE VANITY OF HUMAN WISHES	196
RIDING THE STORM	205
MUSE: LOVE AND WAR	206
ANTHEM	209
THE SUBURB	210
GETTING RID OF MY OLD VIRGIL SCHOOL-TEXT	211
FUISSE / ANDREA ZANZOTTO	212
FUISSE / TRANSLATION	214
THE QUIET MAN	216
POSTCARD FROM N. Y	218
"WHEN LONGING OVERCOMES YOU, SING OF GREAT LOVE" — RILKE	219
FROM A JOURNAL	220

THE LOSER'S CLUB

"History is bunk."

When Mr. A. sat down and stirred his drink,
he turned around to have a word with me:
"The trouble with you, sir, is that you think;
whatever is the use of history?
What will be, will be." I answered, "I agree."

And Mr. B. was listening, and said,
 "That's right, my boy; you've known it all along.
You may as well relax." His face grew red
as though he feared that I'd say something wrong.
My assent soothed him. The brandy burned my tongue.

Then Mr. C., whose chin was rather weak,
sat up and nodded like a beagle hound,
and I acknowledged him with tongue in cheek
by not uttering another sound,
and the whole damned assemblage turned around.

D. hid his mouth behind his hairy hand;
E. winked and asked me if I wanted more;
F. stared as though I were some contraband
and smuggled creature from a foreign shore
whose footprints had just stained the American floor.

I cried, "O Gentleman! I understand —
whatever is the use of history?"
How they crowded round to clasp my hand,

old Mr. G., who has small hope for me,
and even Daddy I., who holds my house in fee.

Reciting alphabets of gratulation —
the opposite of mad Ezekiel -
I struck for luck, and against lamentation,
and they seemed to think that we had saved the nation
when I told history to go to hell.

No wonder history has not served us well.

PROEM

for Janet N. Lembke

The ancient Salian priests were skillful leapers
and danced their songs, quick, adolescent boys
who called the harvest home with ritual hoot
and holler, stamped the foot, and thanked the sun.
They were chiefs' sons, perhaps, the tribe's best brawn,
and never grew old on the job, but were replaced
by the other dancing boys, the best of them,
and theirs were the first songs of the Roman tribe.
Thus poetry, out of the mouths of babes.
It is a need, to bless the blessing sun,
a dance of twelves, a leaping and a singing,
not old man's business, health and happy times,
but better left to boys who grow apace
with the sun's season, time's, time's own golden boys.

But that was long ago. The tribes are gone,
the country cousins, all the pretty maids.
Camenae meant community those days,
when Mused mothered men, and gave them words,
the time to say them, how to sing them out.
That was a time a word could light a world.

It is an old man's trick, this poem of mine,
and I say it to myself, a private prayer
no sage devised, no dancing boy declared,
and it will make no world though it makes me
the way I make it, spare, original,

unique in its own cranky way: my voice
and never yours, though what it seeks
is a reader here and there, enough, perhaps
to make no tribe, but simple following.

And there's the catch! I'm no one-man parade
to march the March with jumping, or halloo
October in, my voice the gathering horn
it takes a host to handle, the full horn
of Cornucopia. I bless myself.

Like that young fellow, singing to his girl
before the college crowd — not an old head
among them — and no ear that knows for sure,
amid the chattering and the coming and going,
that as he lifts his bright eyes up to them
from the typed page, his shoulders hunched and thin,
he's singing for his supper, and not theirs,
and for that neat distinction we all starve.

THE DAY WE DANCED THE SAINT

for Zi' Anton'

The day we danced the saint our shoulders worked
beneath the logs, to the music of a march,
and rowdy with religion we cut loose
to try a jig with that long weight on us,
left flank together, then to the right, the left,
running a little, suddenly stopping dead:
the young girls screamed to watch our statue leap
out of its chocks, it seemed, and lean at them,
his fresh paint flashing in the sun like fire.
The band played *Stella Alpina,* and we danced,
red-faced and grinning; grandmothers cackled back
clutching at their black shawls, and throwing sweets
wide of the mark, crunched beneath our feet.
Where we pushed on small children ran with us,
skipping and hopping, calling a father's name,
Papa Antonio!, like that, in public proof
he held his post beneath the logs that bore
our plaster Saint upon the wooden stage,
where dollars gleamed like sequins on his robe
 and made a noise like feathers in the wind.
Next to me Rodolfo puffed and swore,
his face damp with religion and its work,
while up ahead fat Father Ferdinand
swung with the weight, the Pope's own pachyderm,
"*Laetantur coeli!*" roaring, to our jibes.
"Don't get to heaven too soon!" Rodolfo cried,
and the logs rumbled, but our Saint stayed put.

I glimpsed my mother peering through the crush,
torn between love of Christ, love of her son,
whose skinny shoulders she feared surely would crack
beneath that holy rubble overhead,
but I straightened up, and winked, like some famous athlete,
along with big Arnaldo, Menechin,
Gaetano, Guido, Salvatore and Dino.
We came at last into the smell of wine
and cooking in the air, and the band stopped;
the crowd broke, with a splashing noise, and flags,
shot streamers, colored paper, rained on us,
and suddenly, up front, the old square shone
like a sheet of beaten gold in the noon light.

A young man, like a soldier on report,
raced up to Father Ferdinand, and shouldered
his post with a quick circus-skill that pleased
the elders gathered on the churchyard steps.
The priest walked out, and raised his hands. Shouts back
told him we owned our God that day, at least
and with a smile he signalled to the women
waiting along the ropes, as at a race,
and they ran to us with glasses, cups and flagons,
streaming along the ranks where we stood firm,
squat, sweating Samsons, holding up our pride.
When my girl found me, as I knew she would,
her fingers thrusting mint-leaves in my mouth
and holding up the wine-flask for my kiss,
I was the purest penitent standing there,
and I dared the forty Saints to break my back.

East Rover Nocturne — Felix Stefanile

EXILES

Back home, lost in a crowd, we used to whistle:
direction- inder and darer, the notes
an intricate signal not easily learned,
unmistakable, we'd zero in like sparrows,
a happy clamor of music over the heads
of cops and commuters, the others that were not We,
and — brave as Tonto dying for a friendship —
come scurrying to some corner, some bright-eyed center,

a place to stand, a street to walk, a voice
to answer to, a sign on a face that said You!,
a language, a look, a greeting
with the flick of an eye, the gypsy's nod
that said You out of all the hundreds,
head bobbing, sight clear,
and amid that palaver and shuffle
the trick recognition of tribes;

Love at first sight, Conspiracy.
Need, Profit, Repair,
a committee of cousins. Not interplays of routine
like the chat with the guy on the job,
or the dutiful glance at the little, round behind of the girl in
[the Mail Room,
but instantly a stare and an understanding —
this is where we are, this is what we have come to,
and you and I know where we came from.

East Rover Nocturne — 173 — Felix Stefanile

Now, among the fat cats and pretty frauds,
achievers, functioners, the smug and the smart
doing their thing, their proxy charity
of donation and demonstration,

I'm lost again, in the crown of a college town,
a water-boy to the monks of Education.
They prate like cardinals and preen like crows
while I whistle, like a sparrow, to myself

the Old Religion: what's mouth, what's meant, what's me:
a constellation of nerves and nodes and noise
from the witty creature in the carapace,
red meat of my brain — in its shell
the clam-whip tongue whistling
to the bone scrimshaws of meaning and design —
and the crazily fluted cant
of spine and synapse, my tuneful aerial,

two-footed tuning-fork, thick tine
of my skull held up to catch an answering sound
and hold it up, the fellow-noise, the song
as — singing to himself — the player's played.
I want to hear again the old stadium cheer
of the gang's all here, but all the gang I get
is the chittering in my head of other sparrows,
all up a tree, and no good to me.

We have come to Rome to crumble, a Rome of domes,
an empery of the softly condemned in their circles,
we all come from someplace else, we have all come here —
the foreign snob, the banker's boy from the islands,
the refugee from the candy-stores of Brooklyn,

East Rover Nocturne — 174 — Felix Stefanile

the draft-evader, the charity case, the hop-head,
the man from Washington with his killing machine,
and the slick bombardier of lost causes, the Visiting Poet.

Words, words — Erasmus, what shall I do?
I'm out of breath, like being out of luck.
Where the happy heretics of my laziness flourish
in the slum of my dreams, I hear nothing but whistles.
People are coming and going, coming and going.
Talking. I talk back. Then I move on,
studying my astonishment, like an art.

SLUM

This is the town
where only the young
happen, and in Spring
the streets grow games.

Boys in bright sweaters,
girls with boys' habits
darting in and out
of the traffic, in

tricky machines of flesh,
getting in the way.
Horns warn. Motorists lean
out of windows — they

swear; they feel silly.
Sometimes, Spring is announced
with headlines, like BOY
KILLED BY TRUCK, and

then, though he never
knew their names, we
place wreaths of flowers
on his obedient grave.

ULYSSES ARRIVES

It was not the sea, but my own self,
that harried me. How tell of all the false calms
that so doldrum a voyager can ride
home, like a gull the tide cradles,
the shore awaiting, aglow
with kind weather? What have I come to know?
I have studied the compass of nightmare,
hauled anchor through the yielding kelp of my veins,
drowned sailor, howling awake
toward the diligent dawn. Only now,
with the rigid, heartless splendor of landfall
before me, to stare—caught in the eddies of light
the lean fish of my dreaming—and see
shining in peace the browsing rocks of the headland,
mud's salt smell upon me like a headache,
and hunching over me, old crone, home-town,
scolding me for the drunkenness of my pride
a lifetime ago, that swooned my life away.

EAST RIVER NOCTOURNE

for Michael Yetman

The sun is setting over the dirty channel:
in the slant light the mud glows, soft as suede,
and stinks to holy heaven. Here I am.
I had to sail a thousand miles of grass,
past sky-scrapers of corn grain elevators,
the meadows heaving like a golden main,
to get to where time's all at sea again:
this muck-and-mutter of my childhood home
caught in the mangle of the incoming tide
of old Atlantic, dead, polluted water
swirling under the Queensborough Bridge,
a stream as dark as Styx, as dirty as history.

Back home in Indiana the grand goose goes
like a white sloop, riding a choppy sea
of bean and squash; the tassels clack their dry bells
and the stalks bend their backs in the rolling wave,
their colors changing, roiling in the wind,
the way an ocean changes, green to gray
to flecks of dark and yellow, back to green.
Often, in the soft, mid-western haze
of field and village, an old dream returns,
and I think of this shore, its rubble of broken water,
its haul of cities like bones on a beach,
the cowrie-glimmer of the light, the smell
of grease and smoke, the burning of a world,
and then it seems I've dreamed the corn-fields up.

When I was a boy we swam this cluttered river:
before we dived we called out to our friends,
"Here's half-moon on the Hudson!", and jumped in,
bare buttocks up. Everybody laughed.
Sometimes the girls observed us from the park
a street away, beyond the breakwater.
Their mewing sounded like the complaining gulls
barred from the gleaming flats by the sprawled beast
of our proud adolescence, Pure Disease.
I marvel now that danger never struck:
dead men still ride these waves, the broken glass
glints from the bottoms, bright as Spanish treasure,
the whirlpool of gurgles its gay, drunken song.

The memory is rich, but is it real?
Did something only happen, as is said,
in anecdote, a half-remembered chat
in the gray past, a thing your mother said
you did, until with years the saying made
a certain dream, a memory now yours?
Or did you dream it sure enough one night,
and waken suddenly, amazed with fear,
and then, times later, when the dream came back
it brought no nightmare you could know it by,
and now that you've forgotten you forgot
you can remember, though it didn't happen?
Dreams, fears, shameless fantasies,
the past's that kind of rainbow, dust and light,
a prism for the solipsistic eye,
an art of seeing. The past is bad art;
my art's astonishment, no piety.

East Rover Nocturne — 179 — Felix Stefanile

A nightmare's plenty, we had dreams enough:
we proved our bravery raiding the coal-yards—
fleet of foot, we leaped the barbed-wire fences,
empty coal-sacks fastened to our belts,
and when the old watchmen shook his fist at us,
like Polyphemus, hurled his stones, we hooted,
gathered up the heaps, our boldly harvest.
Or else we raced across the roofs for a glory,
leaping from alley to alley, mountaineers
tilting over the rusty tenement Alps
of pigeon-coop eyries, peaks of pitch and tar.
Once my father chased me up and down
and whaled the daylights out of me. And once
Tully fell and broke his neck. And once
we knocked out all the windows of Platt's Works
on Tenth Street, which was fun, and hard work too.
Sal was caught by Clancy, and didn't snitch;
his father whaled the daylights out of him.
And some weeks later Clancy caught him again
at the cellar-window of the hardware store,
and Clancy whaled the daylights out of him.
That made Sal's father angry. He went to court
to say that Clancy had no right. The judge
said Clancy had no right, and then Sal's father
whaled the daylights out of Sal once more.

Years: wind in a shell, and what's unclean
gleaming, gleaming, ripped fish on a pier,
the half-moon foundered, like a broken bottle,
at the tide's edge, in a rank, glittering place
of horse-shoes, razor clams, the crazy morgue
of an auto-dump, a ziggurat of waste.
Some boys have built a look-out at the top,
a tent of swaying tin. They've hoisted flags

made out of burlap-bags and a bed-sheet,
and scrawled in stolen paint their insolent emblems:
a skull-and-bones, a woman with monster breasts.
This shore's their neutral ground, a no-man's land
to contemplate the world, the dirty sea,
the waves forever rolling toward the land
from what far-flung, untamable beginnings.
They play at being pirates, spy the dogs,
the gulls, the crows, at a calm work of salvage
to glean the pittance that the tide casts up.
There's not a flattery here; they bay like hounds,
whistling and hooting at the strolling cop
who tips his cap at them from a fair distance.

And here I am, without a tourist's eye,
my one good ear not good enough to hear
the siren-flimmer of sentiment's movie-score:
no spirit-lifting floating orchestra
perched in its moon-spot magic helicopter's
technicolor-window zeroes in
on dome and cupola, cosmetic sweep
of arches, bridges, splat geometries
of piers and culverts glossed to satin sheen
in waters lighted by the argon flash
of a saw-toothed horizon blotting out
the nearer stars, and the rich dark of space.
(While the rich hero kisses his slum-days sweetheart.)
Beneath that dome and cupola, that sweep
of crazily canted cables and power-lines
cupping the city in their spider-pouch,
right in the center of the epic, there!
next to the cannery and the soda-plant
that looms like Parthenon by my dim wharf,
off to the side, kink-angled, like a crate

slipped from a truck and splintered in the street,
a patch of window-fleck in the neon's flame,
my childhood home leans to, like shipwreck stalled
in a montage of miracle and mud.

Where is the past to lean to, for connection?
Those Hoosier fields — these corrugated meadows —
my art's astonishment, not piety.
At thirteen Carman tried to kill herself;
"tired of the job," she told the doctor.
Too experienced with death to die
she lived her small death through, and at fifteen
was married, and her child was born that year,
her husband sent to prison. "… for the car.
The car broke down. He couldn't pay for it;
the company was suing him for it.
He forged a check. The baby's all I had,
and that was lonelier than death. I hustled:
I wouldn't go for less than twenty dollars.
It only takes, be nice. You just be nice."
Behind McSorley's Alley, where'd he'd gone
to forage in the junk, as he often did,
an old man found her, among the crates and cartons.
Roses red and yellow at the hem,
she was the flowered dress that caught his eye.

I listened to the hooting of the boys.
All day their rasp is in the city's ear:
the first remark of the gutters, mimic roosters,
they whistled their flags up, hauled their small parades
even before the sun had sense to shine.
They took up all the free seats in my mind
with their gabble on garbage-cans, by telephone-poles,
dust in the wind, cinders to fleck an alley.

They're raucous, and inexpensive, and rather useless,
their cheep as thin as a nail, or a querulous chirping
as of old women out of breath, and scolding.
Lost in the rumble of trucks, the policeman's siren,
their little hordes small matter to the world
and the world — for that — no audience they need
who sing because they sing, and not for supper,
somehow they've made it, made it to the evening,
where searchlights scrawl their tigerstripes in the sky,
and the river, like Ophelia, dances silver.

The Chrysler Building spits St. Elmo's fire
right in my capering eye; across the channel
the sand heaves up its hoard of beer-cans and stars,
and like a council of lost friends, the houses
rise out of shadow, all their helmets gleaming.
A tug-boat's horn, that trails a skein of gulls
to flutter in its wake, like banners streaming,
sounds elegies. The music gets to me —
racked shore, rock-gleam of tides, the creaking pier,
and in my heart these words to answer back.

HOMETOWN

Eliodoro's neon
LEO flickers at midnight from his crazy corner:
lion-whispering nickelodeon.
Leo's legal, has a lawyer;
every winner
needs a warner.

Money-sure
of a public century
Leo dared democracy
and served us all — the Irish, the Negro neighbor,
the pretty mulatto from the U. N.

One trip back, and one night home,
I tried the pizza just for old time's sake —
hot as ever, and the pepper
ground out of an "antiqued" shaker:
Progress had come to the slums.
I missed the ignorant priests and grouchy nuns.

I thought of the public good
as a good man should:
Leo's public face
and the rat-tooth of his public grimace.
I thought of movie-stars
playing tenement mothers, scrubbing clean floors.

When the nickelodeon roared
no saints came marching in.

I swirled toy circles in my gin
and thought of the heart's red eye —
nobody lives forever
and somebody's going to die.

What housing project for the heart?
What suburb for the soul?
The boys were singing "Show me the way to go home"
and I thought of Lorca in New York City
laughing for Whitman
and crying for Rome.

MUSE: TO WRITE IT DOWN

My jangled nerves: the littered table-top
with its wreckage
of books and paper-clips, a fan of notes
spread to the light
like a gambler's hand in a movie.

In the beginning how easy it seemed —
the lucid marble
look of the wood's bare slab
by the open window,
the polished pewter of the sun on a place-mat,

setting me thinking
such calm, such passive glitter
was violable,
and sent me, clomping with packets,
as up to an altar

spread now with pennies, empty match-books, postage-stamps,

and a flame-blackened kettle
fit for no altar,
pouring no nectar.
My table-top is flecked with coffee-stains.

Not the muse drank it down.
Where's my alertness
to recognize pure presence
and wait for help,

not force it?

That would be water,
dizzy as deluge,
and the rainbow-gleam of the dove's wing
shimmering,
the glance of light Noah's bright, cracked transom.

THE WEATHER DIDN'T DO US ANY GOOD

The weather didn't do us any good
that famous winter by the famous sea:
it snowed and snowed. We lived in Noah's city,
or so it seemed — snow was a head-line word,
a terrible miracle. We wished for rain
to wash away the world, and make an end.

It never rained. It snowed and without end,
the air a fog of ermine, and what good —
even the children sang a song for rain
and the gulls sang their words back from the sea.
The wind laughed outright, carrying a word,
and the snow fell, like ashes, on the city.

We moved like mourners, over the buried city
through dirtied paths, in queues, joined end to end
by this new discipline of need, each word
a muttered pass-word for some common good:
we might have been mere slaves, a human sea
locked in emergency. Without the rain

our clever tools were useless, and such rain
as fell turned ice, turned steel. The stricken city
shone icily, a coursing diamond-sea
of peaks and billows, pretty to no end,
where rainbows bared their sabre-teeth. No good
came from the tricky light. The neon word

our beacon flashed was still the same old word.
We read, but never said. Then came the rain,
and washed away the blindness. It was good
to hear the gutters humming through the city,
and watch the snowmen come to a bad end,
and feel the city rising, like the sea,

and shake itself, and shudder, like the sea.
If it was flood we'd suffered through, no word
was written on a wall to tell the end
of anything, because we have this rain,
as steady as the snow, to cleanse a city
not ready for such miracles as do good

when they do good, not bad, to sea or city,
whatever word, like rain, that makes an end.

AMERICAN LEGEND

I

The car, the Great Lakes product,
that leaves Detroit, the squat towns
of the Midwest for villages,
our swimming-pools our alleys—
that clatters past the blinking cross-roads
and shimmering corn-fields from state to state,
clankety-clank,
erector-set of the whistle-stops, its trestles looped
like a huge, mechanical dragon
forever thumping, trundling
its lava-flow of chromium towards the coastlands,
bull-dozing through the counties as flat as money
up to the Alleghenies by dawn,
where the Indian smoke of the light
wreathes it black hump with festoons
of sumac, coiled ropes of the sun—
the car, tin bull, dead coal,
dried spit of fire, whose single urge
is to reach our purgatories of use
in woodlands, museums,
our black dream, fulfilled
only when silence sleeps,
cinder, hissing its hell-tune,
this dead star-splinter, this cold glaze
that answers back the blind stare of our eyes
on the poisonous highway,
it is not the scale of the klaxon serpent
for who we rage,
and that lures us?

II

If you had been a bird, dead racer,
it would have been for the sleepy paralysis,
your head nodding Yes
in your trance of murder by the jack-knifed truck;
(you drove your hearse,
winged like a bird, play-scrap for children in a junk-yard now,
delighted, lost
among the rusted chips of your feathers —)
or if you had been a mole,
as blurred as a star,
nosing your way through the soft dirt of night,
like this rake-combed little body
crumpled on the stranger's lawn,
you cipher on the insurance agent's pad
in a broken kitchen;
(and why not liken you
to the dream-torpedo from Mars
that appeared in the heroin's cupboard
and fell to the floor
clattering like a rainbow?).

It is because the blind ornithologists
have not plucked the jagged feathers
that they never saw your wings,
those flaunting lapels
that bore you through a heaven of motels?
Is it for your shut eyes, that saw nothing,
the tax-payer leaning on his little red sports-car
did not take you for a mole
sneaking towards your subway elysium,
your Zion of underground cables in their nest of clay,
that furrow we tamp now

with the useless instruments of emergency,
a golf club, a torn slat, a flat stone
blasted from the garden wall
at the impact?

If we can only think of you,
shaman,
rattling your tin gourd down the expressway,
deserving the tears of a housewife, the kindness of a cop,
the wide street transformed
into a scenario of a St. Francis of good deeds
(a baby rescued from the flames by a travelling gypsy)
then we shall have our dragon
and his clanking loot,
and you, our Roland,
guarding the pass at Beaver Falls, Pa.,
and for the unwelcome miracle on the lawn
a legend to grieve you.

A CARTOON FOR ARISTOTLE

It is a most commercial hospital:
the calm attendants, dressed in dollar green,
have read the portents of the tinkling pumps
and hand out vitamins of gasoline,
or stand, like patient nurses, at the side
of my black beauty, and stroke his shining hide.

They use thermometers, and probes and lances;
my buffalo's extinct each time he ails.
They serve him the lead-poisons of prescription
and scratch away his coat's infected scales,
and paint him with new salves to hide the fault,
lest with his age, the Age come to a halt.

They take, from cans and boxes in the driveway,
a chipped and broken sun packed in its fat
and stacked like dog food for a snarling motor,
and feed his iron hunger. Marvel at
machines and miracles! that eat the sun,
while we stand by, like priests, to see it done.

Priest or physician, we know no defection,
who led the creature of the silver snout
up to the altar of a clanking clinic,
and drove the god in and the devil out,
past sliding doors and darkness, until here
now, its smoke trails, like incense on the air.

East Rover Nocturne — Felix Stefanile

POEM IN THE MANNER OF
WALLACE STEVENS

for Robert Liddell Lowe

Nothing is the law of the land, sweet dreamer.
Close your dreaming eyes, scan your memory
and of memory be sure, like a philosopher
commending to the Exile who dreams himself
himself another country and patriot,
one man, one vote, and of no other sure.
The simple flaw is that nothing is the law,
sweet dreamer; the mayor of heaven is blind.
Dream, dream then, do your balancing act,
the patriot at one end and at the other
the invincible traitor, the lovely Other,
the true insomniac, the citizen
of that foreign country where dreams keep us awake.
Where's the fulcrum? Where's the acrobat?
Laws are to be obeyed and not obeyed.
In the unkindly land of Schizophrene
we can observe whole armies on parade
before the Commandant who dreamed them up,
the phenom without a name, the man without a country.
Shall we let it be then, let the soldiers stand
in the noon-day sun, like gleaming toys?
The fire-crackers are making a noise
to wake the dead, but the dead obey the law,
and nothing is the law of the land, sweet dreamer:
fix your eye on that thought, like an acrobat.

IN THAT FAR COUNTRY

for Selma

In that far country formed of coves and bays
and clouds that float like swans across the sky,
where nothing happens history can praise
or blame, because there is no history,
I read the sun's handwriting on a wall
of ivied hieroglyphs, I spy a town
where the seasons gracefully return and fall
as in a sanctuary, all my own.
The language that they speak is greek to me
in the still land, where only the children run:
the women weave their nets beside the sea;
the old men suck their pipes beneath the sun,
and people gather in the village square
to ask about me, why I am not there.

ON THE VANITY OF HUMAN WISHES
AFTER THE TENTH SATIRE OF JUVENAL

for Barriss Mills

Search where you will—from Maine to Florida—
observe the antics of grown men at work,
Texas oil-men, New York speculators,
it is the same no matter where you turn:
we study horoscopes and racing-sheets,
seek absolution from our analysts,
or if we court success the classic way
we bet our dollars and our mortgages
on pills, on vitamin-cures, on lotteries.
We make of living one grand traffic-jam
from Washington, D.C., to Disneyland,
and pray for luck and speed, then fall, a prey
to our own gambler's greed. Luck is a lie,
and speed its tricky feet: we get nowhere,
and all that we divine is devastation.
I tell you this, and I'm no fortune-teller.

Where is the soul that is free from pride and error?
We treat the truth like a black man in the slums.
We call it peace, but what we have is war,
and a President is destroyed by its grim power.
We say Prosperity but we mean Plague:
the streams and rivers are dying of our wealth,
the garbage glows like bullion under the sun.
We are as impotent as the stranded whale
choked in its fat off the South Asian beach,

mere blubber-and-oil, a freak of history,
to light the lamps of studious generals
lusting for empery. O false ambition!
is there guerilla war in Monte Carlo?
is there a CIA in Liechtenstein?
As tourists we are warned to watch our dollars—
but nobody robs a peasant of his dollars.
At night we walk the streets, hugging our wallet,
as though it were a baby at the breast.
Poverty grins and whistles in the dark,
and turns its pockets out to show the holes
to any hold-up man who wants to see.
We fear behind the War Lord's back the beggars laugh.

We bribe the pulpit—church or synagogue—
and make meek application (tongue in cheek)
for increase and promotion in man's sight:
do we know the responsibility of riches,
that the gods and goddesses can kill with kindness?
A humble man won't sicken on plain beer:
champagne's the prison, in its crystal cup
that glitters, bright as envy, in our grasp.
Of two old sages, whom shall I commend:
Democritus, who had a sense of humor,
and chuckled every time he stepped outside
and counted the neon-vanities of the town,
or Heraclitus, whose eyes filled with tears?
Laughter is cheap enough: I marvel at
the store of tears that Heraclitus drew from.
Democritus, he almost died of laughing,
yet in his day there were no parking lots,
no generals as college chancellors,
no draft, no Swedish films, and not one moon-shot.

What if he'd seen our Mayor on his Honda,
leading the parade to the town's new pool,
dressed like a Nazi—black and beautiful—
and wearing his helmet like an astronaut?
And what about the band-wagon behind him:
hangers-on, ward-heelers, and the Ward Boss
propped like a mummy in his limousine?
Above us stalked the eagle on the flag;
(for all that, we were sprayed with pigeon-shit).
Then came the mothers, trailing their white crepe,
the children, like tame robots in their stalls,
the local church contingents, the brass band,
the pensioners, the quiet, well-dressed Negroes—
he is their creditor, they are his friends.
His mind poised, like a finger to the wind,
Democritus would have laughed, a real holiday:
small men with big cigars are comical;
in swallow-tails we all of us look like penguins.
He was a country boy, and solid proof
not every hick's a hick. How he'd have laughed—
trouble or trick just one big titillation,
man's tears and joys the same. And as for Lady Luck,
he would have snapped his fingers, told her to "Get lost!"

The Statue of Liberty herself must laugh
at our petitions: favors by the ton.
You pin your dollar to the saint's long robe,
or put a plaque up in the rectory,
it's all the same—Fame, the millstone, drags
the great man down. Fame's perquisite is envy,
and he shackled in a junk of medals.
The climate changes; down the statue comes;
at the city warehouse his furniture is auctioned.
Where's Sherman Adams now, or Bobby Baker?

Nailed to the News. Who are good fellows now?
They're made the butt of a reporter's quip,
the theme of sermons, punch-lines for a comic
a single season; then they die away
like dead-leaves gathered on a compost-heap.

Today you get up early, scoot to town,
and jostle with the crown for a clear seat:
the court-room spectacle is Jimmy Hoffa,
a bull in handcuffs, led to sacrifice—
"… that little tub of lard!" "… but they're all crooks!"
"It's no surprise to me!" "Who turned him in?"
"Who turned state's evidence …?" "Who's getting off?"
A House Committee called him in: *routine*.
The Law's routine's a vaudeville routine.

And what about our *populous romanus?*
It follows headlines, as it always has,
and votes for scandal; and if Lady Luck
had hauled him up instead of dragged him down
it would be cheering him, not jeering him.
Such a celebrity, the gambler's game,
and now that we're a Great Society
our ballots are not worth bribing—citizens
who once struck for the forty-hour week
the union-shop, who balked the Fascist horde,
spend their rewards now on cheap racing cars;
the American Dream is—a long, paid vacation.
Would you be famous, *great*, as Hoffa is,
and draw his salary? Reward your aides
with station-wagons, country cottages?
Be guest at banquets for the Governor,
attend a conference at the White House too?

East Rover Nocturne — 199 — Felix Stefanile

Why not? Think of the pretty go-go girls,
the body-guards, the soft, expensive clothes,
the week-ends in Miami in the winter.
Why not? You needn't wish to rape and pillage
to have that kind of power over life.
But in the grand game that you would be playing,
how many millions worth of fame is worth
the headlong doom that goes along with it?
And would you like now to share Hoffa's cell?
Which would you rather own, Dodd's senate seat,
or the town-stamp at Podunk or Dogpatch,
a Justice of the Peace for traffic fines?
Remember Crassus; better, think of Pompey,
that noble tower looming over Rome,
a veritable mountain-climber of a man
to whom the Alps of fame were women's breasts,
for he sought fame as other men seek Thais.
He lost his head all right; the gods made sure.
There are few kings who live to die in bed;
most get to Hades with holes in their heads.

Our children go to Sunday school, and learn
of famous men (but not how Fame undid them) —
those *servants of mankind*, where are they now?
His very dedication to the peace
struck Gandhi down, who would not raise a hand.
As for that blacksmith's son, born of rude folk,
who dreamed his father's dream of the common man
and clawed his way to power crying Rome!,
he finished on a hook, like a pig's haunch,
derided by the mob. Unfriendly gods!
the boon they grant is as touchy as an asp.

East Rover Nocturne — 200 — Felix Stefanile

And so it is we merit our reward
and earn our stripes, our buttons brass and gold,
our medal's ticket to eternity.
The Purple Heart will buy a purple robe
and lead the State, for mankind dotes upon
the wounded veteran who heals us all.
Ah, Notoriety! What is your gift?
The game's beyond us but we play the game.

The well known congressman, the bold D.A.,
how often has he broken mothers' hearts
to win convictions, send his tumbrils-ful
of prisoners to jail? He makes his mark
and gains new office; with the victory
forgets his old ideals — the War on Crime —
and sits to dinner with the gangster-chief.
Or General MacArthur, think of him,
for whom the crown of Asia was too small.
Called back to his own land, he played the game
of President, despite the President.
Surrounded by old men and foolish youths,
the aged darling of the Gold Star Mothers,
he bore his grudge like Cato, stiff and straight,
sent news releases from his hotel suite
and dreamed of conquest. Poor old Hannibal,
to waste your lion's dotage on coyotes!
He lost that last campaign, a warrior
whose final victory was shame and silence.
What shall we tell our schoolboys of MacArthur?
Remember well the story of Alexander
who had not worlds enough; he's in his cage
of rubble now, the dandelion's slave,
and keeps his court with Xerxes, and the stones.

We, pray, we plot, we dream of a long life;
we make of medicine a time-machine:
a hair-dye will not keep the years away.
Observe the face, as smooth as margarine,
beneath the henna-rinse; she dares not chew
except in nibbles, lest her teeth fall out,
and when she talks she whispers. Her weak voice
is hoarse with age, and like a locust's rasp.
Not all the Floridas in the galaxy
will smooth those wrinkled cheeks, now camouflaged
behind expensive creams. We would live long,
yet only youth has true variety:
the old all look alike, like grasshoppers,
shrill voices, trembling hands, bald heads, sharp knees,
and a terror over food — sighs and complaints.
They are a burden to their families,
and even the fortune-hunter turns from them.
For them the hope of sex is of a gland
as shriveled as a raisin, or a flag
that's at half mast to stay, sad holiday.
What other senses do they have to lose?
They must find joy in watching music sung
for they cannot hear the diva, the sweet harp;
they crouch in the theaters, hands up to their ears,
and tire their friends, who spend the whole night shouting.
Their only hobbies now are aches and pains;
diseases dance around them in a band.
They have more troubles than Venus had lovers
and are encyclopaedias of plague:
one has arthritis, or a hernia,
another one a cataract, a third
has hardened arteries, or half a brain.
Who'd be a bed-case hated by his nurse?
The profit of long life is loss of love;

you bury sons, you're quit of all your friends.
Live long then, and keep chattering to the shadows:
Tithonus, you'll recall, cried for an end.
There's still another side to all of this:
now let the young ones listen for awhile.
Though mothers pray for lovely sons and daughters,
a lad as handsome as John Barrymore,
a daughter prettier than Marilyn,
think how one lived and how the other died.
Such beauty in this world is always fated:
the imperious girl who has no need of brains
will learn, and soon enough, that beauty breaks
as dolls break. There are always other dolls.
What father wants a beautiful son? a clown
who lives off women, only sweats in bed,
and lives a puppet's life, a woman's toy?
Dolls! Toys! Plain girls need no pimps
to find their work for them. Unlovely boys
do all their plowing where it counts, outside
in nature's fields, and will not lack for bread.
Go to it then, proud parents, precious brats.
You'll say to me, "Why not? Latona preened
herself on her Diana's beauty." Yes!
And how about the story of Lucretia?
A rapist's midnight miracle was she,
who was so beautiful she killed herself.
As for that dainty son of yours, reflect
on Nero's preference for such a type;
he never gamboled with cripples, that's for sure,
or buggered after some clumsy, skinny lad.
Your sweet Endymion will die a son
but not a husband. Let it worry you.

"Shall men then pray for nothing?" Who's to say?
I'd leave it to the gods, the good we get,
and what's right in a world we never made;
they know us better than we know ourselves
and deal with us according to our natures.
With us, desire traps. What we call hope
is but a nervous buzzing in the head.
We ask for wife and off-spring; the gods know
the kind we'll get — the kind that we deserve.
Yet if a man would pray, and sacrifice,
and drop his money in the wicker plate,
then let *sound mind in a sound body* be
the miracle he asks for, and a heart
that's strong enough to die, and eyes to see
our days for what they are, mere butterflies
that feed a moment on a morning's gold.
Let him expect no future but hard work;
let him be clam, and curb his appetite.
Let him compete in toil with Hercules,
not dream of junketing like King Farouk.
What I am saying you already know:
it is ourselves that we must truly seek;
we are our own real worth and way to peace.
For want of wit we make of Lady Luck
a sleazy goddess of cheap dreams. The truth
is not so fickle nor so far from home —
we make our luck ourselves, the darling and the doom.

RIDING THE STORM

Safe in my attic
I scan the sky: no danger.
Though the weather turn dark, though the Rockies
rattle the plains with their winds
my house is going nowhere — it is stone,
and the ballast has been tested;
the steeplecock rides like a gull.
Here the winds part like waves to Israel's drumming,
the dreadful miracle hurries past,
we are high and dry.
All that's left is a frenetic whispering,
branches creaking,
a sagging fence-post
that shakes, like a man.
It is quiet again.
I am waiting for the sun
to march down my street, like the mailman,
a little late.

Now is the witching time
of my vigil, the warm, self-confident doze,
when according to legend,
the stranger tries the door
with his knife of silence.

MUSE: LOVE AND WAR

When you look at me
my hands turn proud;
as frisky as two ponies
on ten hooves
they trot up to you.

I wait to be learned
each time you smile at me,
like an ancient cave-drawing
newly discovered
by the torch of your glance,
which is to say
I am the bull offering you sugar.

I become a rustler at your barn,
or you make me a handsome gangster
in a white car
in a grade B movie.
It is permissible:
you make me feel like money.

And I dream of my hope for the world
as a man on a saddle
riding through strange country;
that is the only reason
I call you leather.

But who will polish you in a poem
when I am dead?

I need at least four centuries
to hone you right,
that knife I carry.
The trouble with you
is that
you like to imagine
a landscape of sweet docilities:

                              fennel,
                              those blooms
                              of the squash

that are so hard to remember
and taste so good in an omelette.
This is not the business of the world;
some hard-boiled eggs will do,
though they are not kind.

Now what can you solve
but the pain in my heart?
Who gave you the right?
We have been sad so long
that when you are happy
I feel
like the first days of the French Revolution.
Why don't you stop pitying
our whole ungainly tribe,
and indulging your fancies
about the birds how sweet, lions that lay with lambs?
You need a kid
so you'll stop being mother to worlds,
stop smiling at the people in the bus.

You have no right here.
Go read Kenneth Grahame's *Wind In The Willows*
and go to sleep.

Some day, when the war comes,
they will shoot you first.
That is why I scold you —
forgive me,
forgive me.

ANTHEM

The suburbs, *irredenta,* afflict my sleep.
Priests are hearing confessions on TV.
The moon wastes, like money on fire;
I am amazed at my vote.

O beautiful woman on Channel 2!
Your sweat is as clean as distilled water.
I think of your little son,
the blondest dandelion on the lawn,
who pleaded with me to hate soap. All in vain.
I think of the cop,
that scaramouche of valor,
who poked for a corpse in the garbage can
and came up with a torn brassiere.

Virus be my hobby.
Penicillin my proverb.
Pizza and malted milk for lunch.

THE SUBURB

for Darrel Abel

'tis good, when you have crossed the sea and back,
To find the sitfast acres where you left them.

— EMERSON

Somewhere a robin, like a pulley squeaking
on a wry clothes-line, mars the perfect setting
with his un-abstract noise, but his red's blinked
in a vast gray of street; his nervous feathers

pucker the picture only for a second,
and then the desert whiteness sucks him up.
The lawns run steady in their concrete grooves
bearing the sun's bright, automatic wheels.

It is Etruria, of vanished tongue.
The sparrows shuffle, beggarly old souls,
in a world of stone where all the crumbs are stone,
and the mailman hauls his pouch, like trouble's ghost,

block after block of silence. Or a pedlar,
barbarous as Macedonia,
hoots like a gypsy in the sullen ways,
his exile a mere pock against the sight.

And ever since the country declared health
we build our towns like this, like hospitals,
where all the girls are lean; dogs are taught manners;
and policemen are polite. And even the dirt is white.

GETTING RID OF
MY OLD VIRGIL SCHOOL-TEXT

Popped on the shelf
next to a younger fellow
you lurched, tripped him up,
fell on your side
like a drunk.
I lifted you
with two fingers,
touching gingerly
your wrinkled wings,
and read into you
like a spy in a movie,
afraid my touch
would turn you to powder
spilling all over the floor.

The trash can for you;
the garbageman will cart you off,
light the fire in his rusty drum
with your pages,
an evening at a time,
light of the mind's desire.

You'll do for a quaint holocaust
of old chairs,
lampshades,
dead news like the fall of Troy,
those paper dolls, my saints.

FUISSE / ANDREA ZANZOTTO

Pace per voi per me
buona gente senza più dialetto,
senza pallide grandini
di ieri, senza luce di vendemmie,
pace propone e supremo torpor
l'alone dei prati la cinta
originaria dei colli la rosa
dispersa il sole
che morde tra le tombe.
Ah la cicuta e il poco
formicolio, non più, cola sepolto.
Ah l'acqua troppo tenue che mi cola
oltre la gola e gli occhi e di là di là s'invischia
in tiepidi miseri specchi

su cui l'ortica insuperbisce.
Ed ah, ah soltanto, nei modi
obsoleti di umili
virgili, di pastori castamente
avvizziti nei libri, nella coscia
terrena polvere,
ah ripeto io versato nel duemila.
— Ah — risuona il colloquio
in eterno sventato,
dovunque io passi, ovunque
l'aria mai sfebbrata mi sospinga,
la selva m'accompagni
e impari la vicenda non umana
del mio *fuisse* umano.

Futura età, urto di pietra
sulfureo sangue che escludi
che inintelligibili fai questi
fiori e gridi ed amori,
non-uomo mi depongo
ad attenderti senza nulla attendere,
già domani con me nel mio *fuisse*,
pieghe tra pieghe della terra
cieca ad ogni tentazione d'alba.

FUISSE

Peace to you to me
good people without a dialect anymore,
bereft of the blind hails
of yesterday, the blaze of vintages —
peace is proclaimed and exquisite torpor
by a rainbow of meadows, a prime
circuit of hills, a scattered rose,
a sun
that goes ravening among cemeteries.
Ah, hemlock, and the little thrill
now no more, buried there.
Ah, skinny water trickling
beyond my throat and my eyes and beyond the beyond
mixing in mysteries of mirrors

on which the nettles grow proud.
And ah, an only ah,
for the obsolete custom
of humble vigils, of shepherds
as dry as dust in books,
in the cunning, dusty earth,
and another ah I say,
turned towards the year two thousand,
— Ah — it resounds, the talk
of wasted eternity,
wherever I wander, wherever
the fevered air tells me go.
The forest accompanies me:
I learn the inhuman vicissitudes
of my human *fuisse*.

O age to come, o cry of stones,
o sulphurous blood that vetoes
that uncitizens
these flowers, cries, loves,
I, *golem,* abdicate
to await you with nothing to await,
the tomorrow already here in my *fuisse,*
folds and folds of earth
blind to the least temptations of dawn.

THE QUIET MEN

The quiet men of the noisy streets
touch their hair — you'd think they were girls.
Stepping carefully, for they are cheats,
they wear no hats to show their curls.

From jobs in laundries and restaurants,
shades in a clattering hall,
they stroll and swagger with nonchalance
past your moralities of lysol,

their manners most ulterior
towards maidens of an apple youth.
They have no strength, their cigarettes are bitter,
but their teeth shine like weapons in the mouth.

Their eyes, like pistols, aim at you
to count you for your money;
they nod to your mothers, stiffly, as if to show
they never had any.

More stylish lads, with well-trained hair,
work in banks and wench in quiet.
These, like crucifixes, wear
their knives around their necks and out of sight,

and where they walk, in the darkened town,
rivers seem to sing
and the moon dandles her scarf on the stones
like a lady loitering.

East Rover Nocturne — Felix Stefanile

Policemen hate them cautiously
and club them when they catch them.
They keep their silence, haughtily,
like spies out of Bedlam

aware they sell the Christ they adore,
sure He will outlive them,
but quickly spending their neat silver
before He can forgive them.

POSTCARD FROM N.Y.

Whatever was a Troy that men should
sing of her where no Troy stands?

This town is built upon
History's garbage, and covered with stone,
Indian bones, dried pools,
crumbled Dutch walls
and the ghosts of sea-shells.

in the Portuguese Jews'
cemetery, see, where we fix our clews
amid the brick and steel.
We keep the ocean eel
in the sewers, and he's loyal.

And when the tourists come,
as out of Sparta, any clumsy kingdom,
stiff, and green, and taught
the insolent notion that
Wonder cannot be bought,

the knowing natives sell
with huckster's, barker's, ad-man's ritual,
our cut-rate heritage.
Unbribed, the crazy gull
screams his warning from the Brooklyn Bridge.

WHEN LONGING OVERCOMES YOU, SING OF GREAT LOVE —Rilke

When longing overcomes me I hum to myself
like any good workman, honest, hardly clever,
bending the neck once more, tapping the delicate hammer,
spilling a little ink as thick as blood.

Humming to myself, as I remember
the ruined armadas and the shining water,
the tune in the bell of mud, the conflagrations,
like a virgin with her hand upon her heart,
like an old man with a heart as tough as leather.

And my sorrow lifts her face,
as pure and white as the milk of that first morning,
when she offered me her smile like a knife in the ribs.

FROM A JOURNAL...

... as I wrote to Jim, we are all ethnics indeed, but I mean no easy thing—

We are all exiles. As strangers we raped the Americas. There is the question of homeland, and we left our homes to usurp the homes of the natives. *Can all this count, four centuries later?* Interesting that we call our suburban grids "developments" since we develop little, we only come and go. In our constant settlement and resettlement of the country we have made moving as much a part of our culture as staying put has been a part of the culture of the rest of the world. I think of the brash realtor I know who assures me that a good neighborhood is only supposed to last twenty years. What can he mean?

For around five hundred years now (start with Columbus) one of America's basic functions has been to serve as the arena of settlement of new strangers in place of old strangers—Spanish, French, English and Dutch; Negroes, Germans, Irish; Italians, Slavs, Jews and in our time—Century of the refugee—Jews, Hungarians, Cu- bans, etc. This factor of movement in and out has been charted by our sociologists, but who needs their archeology of dead and dying communities, their charts and graphs and enthusiastic footnotes? Theirs is a science of casualties; we need to name the plague, the dark night that descends on the Inner City of our minds, the ghetto of our souls. That is where the slums have to be cleared.

Because of his history, there reside in the breast of every American two longings: home as a dream of the past, and home as a dream of the future. (Think of Thomas Wolfe, think of the last page of *The Great Gatsby,* that dream of Long Island before the white man arrived!) Since he can't go home again, does he long for a new, ideal home? (Viet Nam? Leisure Village?) Think of Whitman, urging new pieties: "The priest departs, the divine literatus comes." Our dilemma is the present, for we have made a Paradise of the past, and a Paradise of the future. The dilemma is obvious in our historic present—the problems of "neighborhoods" in the cities; the dichotomy of old and young in the nation, as among immigrants, old- and new-line Blacks, and the eternally ubiquitous parvenus of our economically mobile classes; the myth of the South; most currently, the melancholy, if ardent rootlessness of our student generation today.

Against this tragedy set the tragedy of our aboriginal past, the lost chance, the great American desert, Nature as our salvation and doom, destruction of that landscape in search of the landscape of dreams. Ask Pontiac, ask King Philip, those Indians wiped out centuries before "the West was won", Indians our growing boys have never heard of, what future America had. Who then is our Ulysses of Aeneas finding home—Natty Bumppo, Ahab, Huck Finn? Where are you, Ithaca? And what's the symbol, white whale, scavenger gull? History as a gull? Or a robin—Make an epic with a robin, instead of Athena's owl?—the robin William Carlos Williams tells about in his essay *America And Alfred Stieglitz:*

> ... They saw birds with rusty breasts and called them robins. Thus, from the start, an America of which they could have no inkling drove the first settlers upon their past. They retreated for warmth and reassurance to something previously familiar. But at a cost. For what they saw were not robins. They were thrushes only vaguely resembling the rosy, daintier English bird.... Strange and difficult, the new continent in-

duced a torsion in the spirits of the first settlers, tearing them between the old and the new....

That thrush is the past we have murdered. Our Puritan ancestors, they never built the new Zion. And shall we in turn be destroyed by new strangers? Hasn't the palefaced Wasp already joined his Indian victim? Must we remain exiles until such time as history no longer needs America? Is this why we reach out—the sin of our imperialism—pioneers becoming Peace Corps? Is this the circle? Is ours the wrong epic? Will America not be a home until such time as people will not have to leave their homes to seek a home in America? Is America the archetype for modern man?

Glimpses, tatters. Allen Tate, writing of Robinson, his narrative poems especially, says:

> ... Our age provides for the poet no epos or myth, no pattern of well-understood behavior, which the poet may examine in the strong light of his own experience. For it is chiefly in those times that prefer one kind of conduct to another, times that offer to the poet a seasoned code, which have produced the greatest dramatic literature.... The important thing is that [the code] shall tell the poet how people try to behave....

Human failures, yes; tragedy, no. Tilbury town is no Troy. And Roy Harvey Pearce, in *The Cintunuity of American Poetry*, counters with Whitman and Wallace Stevens, and the true Adamic landscape; the battle of Troy is being fought inside the head, the back of the head fighting with the front of the head. He tells us *Leaves of Grass,* the song of the self, is anybody's epic who makes it his, the meaning of democratic man en masse.

Granted my own confusion, I write poems that mutter at the edge of the story, where they may be gathered into the glittering debris left by our underestimated mentors of the recent past—Sherwood Anderson, Edgar Lee Masters, Kenneth Fearing, Theodore Dreiser, Van Wyck Brooks, Trumbull Stickney: *It is raining in the country I remember....* And I get them down: Museum poems maybe, Smithsonian Institute poems, a book that is a flivver of an idea in this age of the unfettered, autobiographical ego in poetry. I take courage from de Tocqueville:

> ... In democratic ages the extreme fluctuations of men and the impatience of their desires keep them perpetually on the move; so that the inhabitants of different countries intermingle, see, listen to, and borrow from each other's stores. It is not only then the members of the same community who grow more alike: communities are themselves assimilated to one another, and the whole assemblage presents to the eye of the spectator one vast democracy, each citizen of which is a people....

And take my own particularity in the absence of those universals whose loss we all mourn, whether we know it or not. "The mythless mind insists that Remus never was," writes Janet N. Lembke in *Arion*; "Megaton technology steals the horror from the javelin and long shield wars.... Venus names a brand of colored pencils and Mercury has wheels rather than winged heels and Vulcan is something one does to Mercury's tires...'" Are specifics, as she writes, capable of generalization? Can our communityless communities forge a vision that works for most of us? Have my poems asked these questions? Are they notes for a kind of epic? I don't know. They do work as a kind of chronicle for me, like that of some lesser, early Roman poet, spying perhaps a god or two among his neighbors, leaving fragments, among so many, for that shaman to come who will name our tribe. May he come, may he come.

In That Far Country

Felix Stefanile

Sparrow Press
103 Waldron Street
West Lafayette, Indiana 47906

Some of these poems first appeared in the following publications: *Commonweal, Elizabeth, Grillo, Hap, Occident, Penny Poems from Amarillo College, Poetry Chap Book, The Spokesman* (Loras College), and *Yankee*.

'In That Far Country' appeared in *The New York Times*, (c) 1959 by The New York Times Company. Reprinted by permission.

'Girl in the Garden' first appeared in *The New York Times*, (c) 1962 by The New York Times Company. Reprinted by Permission.

'A Song for Rory' appeared in *Poetry*. Reprinted by permission.

'It Rains in the Neighborhoods of Epiphany' appeared in *Poetry*, (under the title 'In the Sea's Alchemies'). Reprinted by permission.

'Sonnet 3' appeared in *Umberto Saba: 31 Poems*, published by Elizabeth Press. Reprinted by permission.

Copyright (c) 1982 by Felix Stefanile

ISBN: 0-935552-14-6

Listed in the index of American Periodical Verse
Typesetting and production, Tom Montag, *Midwestern Letters*

In That Far Country

For My Dark Lady

You are my head-line; let men threaten war
and poison all the rivers of the air!
I know my own importance—it is you;
I do not fool myself with history.
And let them read the poor moon's frozen mind,
the idiots. I handle your slim bones
like instruments, and steer the galaxy,
a lucky fool who does not lack for fuel.

The earth revolves around me when you do:
then I become like Ptolemy's mote, and dare
the universe's might, proud of my dust,
and ride the stars, you my astronomy,
where the Twins bound, and the Crab tears his house,
and my own astronaut, the Ram, runs on.

A Word to Maecenas, in His Park

Above the careful shadows of the town
the moon moves, as discreetly as the dream
this statue, underneath her formal beam
might entertain, and still not lose the frown
some hired artist gave him with his gown
out of a prejudice to make him seem
engrossed in some important, civic theme,
and put him looking stiff, and looking down.

All the expensive silver of that light
goes wasting on our proud and settled tribe
who've long forgotten when the last moon shone
that was not but a symbol of space-flight,
or Beauty, that was not a kind of bribe,
or Statues, dreaming anything but stone.

The Girl in the Garden

inscription for a Cook-Book

Here is a garden: in the morning light
the path glows smooth as pewter where she stands
with gathered fruit like baubles in her hands,
all streaked and silvered from the dews of night.
On a high branch a sparrow, full of fight,
accuses her and her bright contrabands;
I dream my dream of calm and quiet lands
where every girl and bird is just as bright—

where the wide table, like a banner spread
a harvest-blazon shows: heraldic grain
the lover and beloved share as one;
where bold as bullion glows the golden bread,
and, lost in thought and grateful for my gain,
I watch birds fly my poems to the sun.

A Song for Rory

from "Some Songs for Billie Holiday"

Think of Rory sleeping on the table
and dreaming of his fortyleven windows,
shoulders hunched, like a jockey in a stable,
still riding gargoyle past the judges' windows.

A crazy wino crying soft and steady,
whose fingers prayed to rein his horse of lust,
while over the sprawled lumber of his body
the sun ran like a spider in the dust.

Remember how the nickelodeon roared
like a wrong lion, and shook up his dream?
And he banged his head against his bed and board
until the very wind began to scream?

And for his bane's brawn, and his belly's fight,
cops offered mercy, lodging for the night.

You, Poet, in Your Garden

You, poet, in your garden, where you doze,
or like a prophet pondering the times
inscribe a sermon on a "towering oak,"
what simple mews makes you so comfortable?
Here they are brave enough, my pocket-parks:
a cantankerous sapling bursts its wired prison:
the privet, tough as plumbing, full of turns,
tugs at my sleeve with a persistent gesture.

The wind's horn rides bone fields down my bare sight
to where the El, like Stonehenge, flares at dawn—
no moral but the climb I have to make.
I show my age upon these rusty steps,
but that means blood of iron—I should know;
I grew where oak trees have no strength to grow.

It Rains in the Neighborhoods of Epiphany

In the sea's alchemies the visual sun
sinks like a whale, churning kinetic gold.
The veering gulls tear at my sight like a game,
and in the private poverty of my life
I hear for the first time the noise of myself.

You must fear the water to learn the Bible's navy:
how Noah swam the seven alcohols
breathing a proper dread. Sailor, be like the fish.
Turn to that shelled mother of the world
who wore you like a wound once, slipped you in water.

There sings us low a zodiac-spinning wind
that named the gods. They wore no moral stitch,
but made the world. Sailor, say Land! like a flag,
your guilt has gills. Your Noah was a fish.

Paradise

From the Italian of Umberto Saba (1883-1957)

There comes to me in dreams a little house
on a steep hill, surrounded by an air
of pure serenity, and brightly there
the hill's green stands apart: blest is the hour.
There comes to me in dreams a little goat
that follows me, and slyly, calmly stares,
my peaceful, fellow being. We form a pair
drawn to each other. Then she chews the grass.

The sun is setting: on that house set high
and solidarity, a gold splendor gleams
set off by windows shining in the light.
And all the sweetness that abides in life
to that sole pitch, to that one lingering flame
has now arrived, and to that last good-bye.

American Aubade

A crazy cardinal
is sitting on the fence: he sings
to the whole town, and counts us house by house.
We wake up to wisdom, as he brings
news of chores to all, and in a madrigal
pure yodel and carouse
daylight's plain reasoning
to anybody's dream.

Is his a music verse cannot declare?
All who had slept and started turn again
in a dawn honed by bells, as on the air
his red and sequin clapper startles them,
the taunt and the refrain,
toward wines of color that the windows wear.

Dawn

Dawn:
the Word saying itself
once more,
like a sign on an awning.

I stand by my window as by an easel,
while the hours shape themselves
somebody's pipe,
a scampering squirrel,

clouds as white as laundry on a line,
and the sparrows
starting to live it up,
to evening, I think.

I'll make it, make it, maybe,
put it in a poem.

Hometown

The drunks sang hero to the moon, that like
a bill-collector, stalled along the streets,
wishing my old man home. A concrete lake,
the warehouse glittered under the wind-swayed lights,
where a policeman stepped, head bowed and whistling,
amazing the silence with his loneliness.
The dawn came grayly, with the gulls,
the slow ruckus of the milk-truck, and my mother
padding, a sheeted figure, to the door,
opening to a cold, tin foil horizon.
The bottles she gathered rang like a white money;
the church-clock clanged with a country tongue;
the sparrows clicked like pennies on the pavement,
saying the world was round again, like her.

On the Vanity of Wisdom

In the apple-green library room, pungent
with floor-wax, the smell of soap from young bodies,
I took my seat and shuffled my ancient
text. The print danced on the page like flies.

I listened, almost dozing, to the hush of homework
down the long table. Then a book slammed shut,
a girl stood up, God knows why, a smirk
on her face, young breasts bobbing, and put

a finger to her lips, smiled us down.
She gathered her things; her long hair swayed like a fern
by a pool, as she tossed her beautiful head

and glided past us, levitating I swear
like Aphrodite. She gave us quite a turn,
but I hope she remembered her date, and got it on.

Landmarks

> *Written to commemorate a court ruling that the Good Shepherd Church of West Lafayette, Indiana, now no longer in use, is not a landmark, hence freeing the new owners of the property to proceed with their plans to raze the edifice.*

There was a time, when travelling east of west,
as once our old explorers did, a man
could quit, turn back, and find his spot again,
and hug his corner, in his memories rest.
Now turn your back and wander, at the best
you'll voyage home a stranger and has-been,
your town paved over, Progress wiping clean
the landscape in your head you thought would last.

DuBellay wrote a sonnet about home,
preferring it, he said, to mighty Rome;
his little cottage fitted like a shoe,
and better than empire was his dear Anjou;
better than Tiber was his gentle stream,
along whose shore now condominiums gleam.

The Old House

There's the old house, a ruined fort
tilting and sinking in ash and dirt,
burrowing into the immitigable
smoke and soot of another dayfall:
peeling, weed-stopped, windows boarded,
graffiti in Spanish and English, loaded
words that speak of history,
but only tell the world to die.

Look again. The pigeon builds
her nest on an abandoned sill,
and broods and broods unconscionably,
instinct with posterity.
The meek shall inherit a little longer;
lovers still whisper in their rumpled beds.

On Family Quarrels

from the Italian of Cecco Angiolieri (1260?-1312?)

The little kid returns unto her kind,
though she may scamper for a while away;
sons and fathers beat each other blind,
and brothers brothers' blood draw in the fray,
and uncles, nephews, their own cat-love find,
and wife and husband clout the livelong day,
yet for all families to war inclined
will come their peace, with little left to pay.

Therefore, I warn, let no man interfere
with people so conjoined. If he discerns
the knife-wound even, let him never stare,
for blood is very strict in its concerns,
and though pure wrath consume them, gathered there,
unto her kind the little kid returns.

*Benedetto Croce, in his book on popular poetry and court poetry, makes special mention of this sonnet: "...it has the tone of a modest commentary on some proverb, and yet there's more to it – an insight into humanity, illumined by a warm smile, that in that proverb finds its true expression; a ditty, but a lively ditty that in the closure, returning on itself with a little inversion, resembles the little goat herself, wandering back and forth, and quite satisfied with herself..."

Marty to Marian

I'd like ta know who needs this kinda night:
she's standin' at the winda, lookin' out,
an' if I talk now she'll just turn an' pout
so I keep quiet. She puts out the light
an' tells me that the moon's as calm an' bright
an' around as Heaven's dome, I don't dare doubt
cause she says so, so I just let 'er spout,
like poetry. Me, it's ole bones, that white

ole bony moon, an' nothin' I can thank.
She's got more moon 'n 'at moon has, I swear,
but she's just wastin' it, an' that's a sin.
I just lay back, an' I don't fuss or crank —
the moods she gets sometimes I wouldn't dare —
but man o man o moon! the mood I'm in.

After cummings

o you who are so anytime most fair
as sleeping virgins in the still, jade lands
of all time's aprilpast, and whose slight hands
(this way I kiss) that, ordered like a prayer,
lie like a clasp to bind your burnished hair;
you whose lips form questioning allemandes
for my allegros, as Love moreso stands
than statues will their marble beauty wear,

so too many swift enchantment will abide
beyond incredible thieveries of our doom,
and though my love be child of stumbleart,
yet were Death very running, I should hide
(and all my bones laugh in their velvet room)
the impossible red pennies of my heart.

Sonnet 3

from the Italian of Umberto Saba (1883-1957)

My father, *assassino*, so I thought,
until I met him on my twentieth year,
and knew him for the child he was, and saw
that for the gift I have I have him clear.

My own blue stare upon his face I caught;
a smile, for all his troubles, ear to ear.
Forever the world's pilgrim: what he sought,
by more than one girl nourished and found dear.

He was a gay one and light-hearted; my mother
felt every weight and burden of her life.
He slipped away from her like a balloon.

She used to warn me, "Don't be like your father."
I understood it in me later on:
they were two races at an ancient strife.

(from "Autobiografia," *Autobiography*, 1924)

* *Saba's father abandoned his wife before the poet was born. Saba did not meet his father until he was twenty. The "ancient strife"* (antica tenzone), *is a basic theme with Saba of a family divided. His mother was Jewish, his father Gentile.*

Gossip

Words are more than words. Speak of the devil
and he shows up, the uninvited guest
in your own garden—dressed, perhaps, to kill—
spoiling the brittle talk. A butterfly dangles.
Hollow rejoinders, if you like, now toss
in summer's shimmer to a sigh of pines
amidst which, here and there, a sudden breeze
lifts up a sleeve of light. Then shadows fall.

The afternoon is blameless, but not you.
You offer chair and cup to your wrong guest,
who as he sips now smilingly looks up
as though to say you did not taste the brew
before you offered it, but he will drink.
You both are poisoned by hypocrisy.

Lines From a Poet in Residence

A thousand miles of lawn separate
me from my home; my sport shirt gleams like golf
in the expensive sun. The slums are dark
with smoke and despair, but I am not
despondent. I am here. I am safe.
My muse was once as saucy and as tough
as any other dude on those dirty walks:
I was poor. I was out of a job. What poems I wrote,
Leuconoeh, on your hair, your slender hands,
the days we poured Provence and Tuscany
on the kitchen table. How the memory aches—
you said my poems were the wine. Now whiskey
pours, as bitter as profession, and yet once
I twittered like a canary, on unemployment checks.

* The heyday of the sonnet was probably the late thirteenth and early fourteenth century in Italy. This was the period of the great sonnet cycles of Cavalcanti (who inspired Pound), Dante, and Petrarch. It was the time of a poetic "revolution" the Italians refer to as *il dolce stil nuovo,* "the sweet new style." A major characteristic of that style was the poem honoring the Lady who, in various guises was Queen of All Hearts, the prefiguring Angel of Heaven above (Laura, Beatrice), and general Enchantress. What Italian poets did, to great effect, was to Platonize the earlier Lady of the poets of Provence and set her on a pedestal. This philosophical impulse seems a natural outgrowth of the medieval cult of Mary. That the tradition had great power—much abused by inferior poets—is evident in its influence through the centuries. In England Shakespeare, three-hundred years later, felt called upon to ridicule the blowsier aspects of this tradition in his sonnet CXXX (*My Mistress' eyes are nothing like the sun...*).

What follow are one example of "the sweet new style" and our Grand Lady, and some spoilsport rejoinders by the scamp of the whole *stilnovisti* movement, Cecco Angiolieri. His sonnets, replying to Cavalcanti and Dante, indicate among other things how well a sonnet can be turned to polemical purposes.

On the Mightiness of Love (Sonnet I)

from the Italian of Guido Cavalcanti (1255?-1300)

You, who through my eyes have reached my heart,
and wakened there a mind that had been sleeping,
observe now all the torment which, sighs leaping,
Love overtakes, as I am torn apart,
with such a strength he comes and cuts, to start
my failing senses out of their own keeping:
it is a new face that I wear for weeping;
with a new voice I cry aloud my hurt.

This feat of Love that has undone me came
from your own noble eyes, whence cunningly
he loosed the dart that entered in my side;
I felt him strike the moment he took aim,
and now my soul's ashiver, stunned, to see
the slain heart in my breast I must abide.

* *To us Cavalcanti is perhaps best known as the author of a poem written in exile, the first line of which became, in English, Eliot's "Because I do not hope to turn again" from "Ash Wednesday."*

Advice to a Courtly Lover

from the Italian of Cecco Angiolieri (1260?-1312?)

You, Ciampol, taking long looks at that crone,
who moves so queerly, with a puckered frown,
and stiffens as she struts, pure skin and bone—
her odor guarantees she'll stand alone—
and fidgets like a monkey on her throne,
so is her face and figure up and down,
and simpers as we watch her, smooths her gown,
and twists and moves her mouth as round a stone—

it's wrong of you such moods to undergo
of wrath and anguish, love's and fancy's darts;
little pleasure comes to you that way;
yet you've been marveling at that dame all day
until her spell's enough to stop the flow
of kindly feelings in romantic hearts.

A Critique of Dante

from the Italian of Cecco Angiolieri (1260?-1312?)

Dante! comrade Cecco now must send
a word, beseech you as he would a lord,
and by the god of Love — whom you've adored
a long time also — his own cause commend,
and beg your pardon if he should offend;
such surety your kind heart can afford.
The matter that I treat's here underscored —
in short, I find fault with your sonnet, friend.

The way I see it, and your "turn" depicts
a gentle spirit is addressing you
whom you don't understand (by Beatrice!).
But then you tell the dear ladies that you do,
and verily the one verse contradicts
what in the other verse you said was true.

* *This sonnet attacks the last sonnet (and the last poem) of Dante's "Vita Nova." It is a poem that Dante explains even more minutely than usual in that book. Italian scholars, like d'Ancona and Contini, have conjectured particularly about this comment on Dante's sonnet. The "turn", of course refers to Dante's sestet.*

In That Far Country

for Selma

In that far country formed of coves and bays,
and clouds that float like swans across the sky,
where nothing happens history can praise
or blame, because there is no history,
I read the sun's handwriting on a wall
of ivied hieroglyphs, I spy a town
where the seasons gracefully return and fall
as in a sanctuary, all my own.
The language that they speak is greek to me
in that still land. Only the children run;
the women weave their nets beside the sea;
the old men suck their pipes beneath the sun,
and people gather in the village square
to ask about me, why I am not there.

Postscript

Some time ago I wrote that in our liberated age perhaps the only avant-garde thing left for a poet is to compose a sonnet sequence, written preferably in the Italian vernacular, and dedicated to Laura. Everything else had been tried, and the sonnet might qualify as an experiment "not being done." Of course people still write sonnets, poets like Marilyn Hacker, William Bronk, Howard Nemerov, Hayden Carruth. The sonnet is a remarkable survivor, and as writing is over eight hundred years old. As early as 1332 one Antonio da Tempi included a discussion of the sonnet theory in his *Summa Arti Rithmici*. I think it is correct to say, however, that most of us consider the sonnet a form hopelessly dead. A long time ago William Carlos Williams, with a clouded look on his handsome old face, told me so, and he had been saying that to young poets for years. I answered, "No! the sonnet isn't dead, but people writing sonnets are." He turned away for a moment, as much as to say *that* discussion was finished. I made no attempt to labor the point.

In the light of the foregoing anecdote I leave it to the reader to surmise the real state of my personal health. As for our mistrust of composition and structure, it is the going platitude in all the arts. The air is full of talk about the process of the poem, the material just "happening" on the page, organic form. In our neo-Romantic gusto we have carried Keats's accidental injunction in a letter, about negative capability, to the extreme limits. I have heard poets seriously say, in their concern for the pure moment drifting towards them and through their thoughts — like a breeze gently agitating the windchimes (Aeolian harp?) on the front-porch—that they never, or hardly ever revise. I think to myself, How wonderful!, and it all makes me feel very stupid.

There is Croce's simple and perceptive remark about the sonnet, that you only notice the form in bad poems. An ideal is implied in such a remark. Is that ideal so very different, in execution, from the inspiration Babe Ruth had one legendary day at bat, when he pointed to where he would hit his home run, and then proceeded to knock the ball out of the park? Was that feat magic, or like most miracles, hard work? Isn't all inspiration, all purity of the organic form, all "success" of this kind, whether in art or sport or just doing your job well, a matter of being *ready* for the moment, rather than the moment? And how do our saints of both East and West tell us to be ready? By patience, by ritual (which is practice), by emptying ourselves of distraction so that we are alert to chances, in short by the devotion that keeps one playing baseball (or trying to write poems) all one's life in the hope of hitting home runs. (As for not revising, I must confess it helps to start by being Shakespeare.)

The small collection of sonnets here presented attempts no sequence, no single theme. In time the pieces are gathered from about 1957 to the present. Some of them have been revised since publication, a couple drastically so. (All forms make for tinkering, and I enjoy tinkering.) Yet I have let stand an earlier, opulent work or two—the poems are not in chronological order—in the dim hope that, among other designs my pamphlet might serve the right young, or inexperienced reader as a text of sorts concerning the vicissitudes of rhetoric and composition. I hope my efforts to "ring the changes" on the sonnet form are not too obvious.

My impulse for setting forth with this little book is clear to me: I'd like these sonnets, compiled over the years, to be in one place. I also happen to think this is an apt time for such a modest venture. Our subscription for these pamphlets has never been better, and I am assured of a few readers. Also the weather for poetry is mixed up these days, and Experiment itself is no longer the totalitarian tornado it appeared to be a few years ago. Nostalgia is in the air, and a new tolerance for the past, as we note the horrible future we have made of the present. I must also add that the sheer novelty of coming out with a collection of sonnets — and my own at that, the only one I had at hand — appealed to me. This sort of "newness" (and unavailability) is what the little magazine is about. (I invite the scholars to check into just how many sonnets are being published in these times, this generation.)

Instead of beginning this note with an epigraph, I decided to end with an apograph—

> No! Time, thou shalt not boast that I do change;
> Thy pyramids built up with newer might
> To me are nothing novel, nothing strange;
> They are but dressings of a former sight…

Shakespeare, Sonnet CXXIII

Felix Stefanile

June 11, 1982
West Lafayette, Indiana

About Our Series

The *Sparrow Press Poverty Pamphlets* are a continuation, in different format, of the *Sparrow* magazine, established in 1954. The new *Sparrow* features, in each issue, the work of one poet. Recent Sparrow Press poets have rated essays and reviews in *America, News Art, Indiana Writes Newsletter, Parnassus,* the *Pikestaff Forum, Slow Loris Reader* (no. 3), and *Modern Haiku.* We have also, over the years, received mention in *Nation, Poetry, American Scholar,* etc. Sparrow Press considers its pamphlet series, as well as its other books, a forum for committed poets of sustained achievement. Subscription to the series, at three issues a year, is $6.00.

Back Issues of Sparrow Available on Microfilms

Arrangements have been made with University Microfilms of the Xerox Corporation to provide a full run of back issues of *Sparrow*. Please order from University Microfilms, 301 N. Zeeb Road, Ann Arbor, Michigan 48106

The Dance at St. Gabriel's

poems by Felix Stefanile

The Dance at St. Gabriel's

Story Line Press & Peterloo Poets

1995

© 1995 by Felix Stefanile
First American Printing

All rights reserved. No part of this book may be reproduced in any form or by any electronic or mechanical means including information storage and retrieval systems without permission in writing from the publisher, except by a reviewer.

Story Line Press; Three Oaks Farm; Brownsville, OR 97327

Peterloo Poets; 2 Kelly Gardens; Calstock, Cornwall PL18 9sa U.K.

This publication was made possible thanks in part to the generous support of the Nicholas Roerich Museum, the Andrew W. Mellon Foundation, the National Endowment for the Arts, and our individual contributors.

Book design by Chiquita Babb

Library of Congress Cataloging-in-Publication Data

Stefanile, Felix, 1920-
The Dance at St. Gabriel's : poems / by Felix Stefanile
    p. cm
ISBN   1-885266-08-1
1.   Italian Americans — Poetry.   1. Title
ps3569. T339D36   1995
811'.54 — dc2o   95-6896
                                      cip

Acknowledgments

Some of the poems in this book were originally published in magazines, and elsewhere. I note the publications that follow with gratitude: *Canto, The Centennial Review, Elizabeth, Footwork: The Paterson Literary Review; Kayak La Fusta, The Lyric, Modern Age, New Letters, The New York Times, Occident, Poetry* (Chicago), *Poetry Broadside, Poetry Now, River City Review, Saturday Review, The Sewanee Review, The Sycamore Review, Yankee.*

The two translations from the Italian of Umberto Saba were originally published in *Umberto Saba: 31 poems,* issued by the Elizabeth Press in 1978 with the permission of Linuccia Saba, ("Ulysses," and "The Boy and the Shrike"). "The Dance at St. Gabriel's," title poem, was originally published in *From the Margin: Writings in Italian Americana,* published by the Purdue University Press in 1991. "Driving East, Thinking of Frank O'Hara" was originally published in *Voyages to the Inland Sea, VIII,* University of Wisconsin LaCrosse.

Contents

I. The Dance at St. Gabriel's   267

On Theory and Practice   269
Grandfather's Story   270
The Light-Bringer   271
Hanging Out   272
The Catch   273
The Americanization of the Immigrant   274
December, 1941   275
The Dance at St. Gabriel's   277
Soldiers and Their Girls   278
Edie   279
Ballad of the War Bride   281
L'Ultima Rinunzia   282
Ballade of the Sad Celebrities   283
Rewriting the Cagney and Lacey Show   285
Some Mentors:
    1.   To Answer Robert Frost   288
    2.   Cheering Amy Lowell On   289
    3.   Taking Sides with John Ciardi   290
Driving East, Thinking of Frank O'Hara   291
On a Remark by the Poet, Dana Gioia, on Translating   293
At the Widow Kate's Retirement Banquet   295
Spoiled by All My Tyrants   296
The Marionettes   297

II. The Bocce Court on Lewis Avenue   300

III. Geographies   313

The Old Clothes Tree   315
Midwest Fantasy:
    1.   Winter: Red's Barbershop   316
    2.   Spring: The Mourning Dove   316
    3.   Summer: August   317
    4.   Autumn: Indiana   318

The Hunters	319
On Painting a Bike	320
From an Apartment House Window	321
Binary Rhymes	322
Irises	323
The Insect World	324
The Motel at the End of the Ramp	325
Andrew	326
The Metaphysics of Winter	328
Umberto Saba:	
Ulysses	329
The Boy and the Shrike	330
Elegy, 1942	331
Hubie	333
Honorable Army Discharge	339
The Veteran	340

When we journey into life it is in the company of a good angel, who has been bestowed on us in the guise of a close companion. Even those of us who do not sense the good luck this companion brings will nevertheless feel a deep loss the moment the border is crossed from our country, when the angel forsakes us.

The Brothers Grimm

adapted from a translation by Robert Ward

These poems are for Selma.

I.

The Dance at St. Gabriel's

> I am a child of the Depression,
> and no one can take that away from me.
>
> *Marion K. Stocking*

On Theory and Practice

To make the familiar strange, that is a touch
that can anoint, that can transform the self.
Make the strange familiar, agitate
the consciousness. Then everything you feel
is revelation. What is tame is shame,
the absence of a probing mind. Forget
all talk of contours, and accomplishment
of right surprise will lurk at every hand.

How hard he tried, Van Gogh, in, out of touch
with his familiar lump of world and self:
his daubs and scrapes and scratches agitate
the consciousness. Old Shoes. And yet you feel
the world's accessibility as no shame,
though acceptance is a doze. Forget
the laziness of fact. Accomplishment
is the old brush that trembles in Van Gogh's hand.

Grandfather's Story

My mother bathed me in warm wine
for I was weak and puny at my birth.
The wine kept me alive, and I grew stronger.
My father warmed the wine
with a horseshoe burned red hot.
Thus I took in the cleverness of wine,
the endurance of iron.
To cool me then my mother cradled me
in the new leaves
of a blooming chestnut tree.
Soft, soft was the touch,
and I slept mightily.

The Light-Bringer

A little kitchen: in the window's gloom
the coal-stove goes on purring like a cat
with one lid slitted open, crescent eye
casting its livid wink into the hall.
My father enters, holding in his hand
a mantle, as we called it in those days,
a small hood of wire-mesh to snug around
the gas-jet on the wall. I'm there somehow,
staring with all my might. He slides a chair
against the wall, climbs up, and does his trick
of pulling out a match and striking it
against his pants leg. It hisses, spurts alive.
I understand my part. I clanked the stove-lid
back into its flange. Everything turns dark
except for match-light, and the tiny star
that twinkles in my father's eye. But I
know what will happen next. The mantle glows,
and as he turns the jet the flame grows full,
the kitchen blooms with light, darkness dispelled
then he hops down, whizzing the chair towards me
with a sudden grin. The window pane is gleaming.

Hanging Out

Standing on corners, waiting for the girls,
smiles on our faces, holes in our shoes,
we whistled and the sparrows whistled back.
The moonlight lay like cracked glass at our feet.

Standing on corners, waiting for the girls,
our blood did all our thinking for us then.
Beans for brains, as poor as pigeons,
who was it that worked steady in those days.

Standing on corners, waiting for the girls?
The wind, like a cop barking, kept us in line.
We stepped between the puddles as we walked.
What happened to the girls? The girls ran home.

The Catch

Your college learn you be smart, talk fancy. You go with the girls, talk fancy. You tell your mother, Ma, why you got the bun on your head, old fashion. Your college learn you don't respect your mother. Some college. Now you say this girl you live together, marriage never mind, old fashion. Your mother cry, and with the beads pray pray and pray. What you think, she ask me. You know what I think, boy? I think if you was pig we raise by and by we sell you for money now, not your mother cry.

The Americanization of the Immigrant

Your words, Genoveffa,
through the open window,
telling me once again
what to buy at the store —
don't forget, don't forget —
aroma of fresh bread
almost a halo.

That was a long time ago.
I never forgot.
Like Dante
I have pondered and pondered
the speech I was born to,
lost now, mother gone,
the whole neighborhood bull-dozed,
and no one to say it on the TV,
that words are dreams.

December, 1941

Pearl Harbor week: the campus in a frenzy,
and the Dean calling chapel every day
so we could listen to the dignitaries
entrained from Washington, or Fort Somewhere.
Loudspeakers sprouted from each corner lamp-post,
reminding us of Hitler's Germany;
recruiting booths sprang up in all the squares,
and the Marines stood guard by Lincoln's bust.

In Latin class but five of us showed up
to meet with Halliday, grumpy as usual.
The bell rang, and he started to call roll
when Melton entered, walking on tip-toe,
a wide grin on his chubby face. He clattered
getting go his seat, and Halliday
stared at him, thanked him for his kind attention.

Melton burst out, "I'm switching. I've just been . . ."
He babbled on about V-8, V-12,
and other officer enlistment programs
now opening up, with schooling guaranteed,
and then a little hitch in the Reserve
if war was over when he finished training.
He seemed to need confirming, kept it up,
"I'm going to dental school; it's a good break,
I'll wind up a commissioned officer."
What this amounted to was a three year deferment.

Old Halliday let loose his glare and grunted,
"I'm happy you're so ready to do duty."
Our small group stiffened. Melton was an ass,
and Halliday no help. No wisdom there
that nasty, frigid, gravel-colored day.
We looked down at our books, and shuffled papers.

Years later, in a tavern—it was peace time,
though U.S. troops were fighting in Korea—
I bumped into Don Mills, a fresh M.A.,
just out of college through the GI Bill.
Immediately he told me about Melton;
he was in South Korea, pulling teeth.
We grinned and grinned, and bought each other drinks.

The Dance at St. Gabriel's

for Louis Otto

We were the smart kids of the neighborhood
where, after high school, no one went to school,
you NYU and I CCNY.
We eyed each other at St. Gabriel's
on Friday nights, and eyed each other's girls.
You were the cute, proverbial good catch
just think of it, nineteen—and so was I,
but all we had was moonlight on our minds.
This made us cagey; we would meet outside
to figure how to dump our dates, go cruising.
In those hag-ridden and race-conscious times
we wanted to be known as anti-fascists,
and thus get over our Italian names.
When the war came, you volunteered, while I
backed in by not applying for deferment,
for which my loving family named me Fool.
Once, furloughs overlapping, we met up,
the Flight Lieutenant and the PFC;
we joked about the pair we made, and sauntered.
That Father Murray took one look at us,
and said our Air Force wings were the only wings
we'd ever earn. We lofted up our beers.
Ah, Louis, what good times we two have missed.
Your first time up and out the Germans had you,
and for your golden wings they blew you down.

Soldiers and Their Girls

(First Three-Day Pass)

Those years before Fast Food a pizza meant
a neighborhood, an accent maybe, or
the way the customers looked. You had your limits.
One train-stop more it might be Fish and Chips

or Blintzes. What a way to spend a date,
skipping from joint to joint, and getting drunk
on laughter and strange sipping, stupid jokes
about the squid, rose-water, or flat bread.

Whatever, down it went. You smiled and smiled
because the girl was pretty and was proud
and scared. She wanted you to know
Armenians were just like you, or Jews,

and we were all Americans anyway.
You checked your watch, said "Hitler!" She teared up,
pert Rosie Ohanessian, whose large eyes
were darker than that last night on you mind.

She walked you to the depot. You held hands,
but never made a move, the station crammed,
young couples slouching, grinning, waiting for
the speaker to announce the bus from camp.

Edie

        Rockingham, N.H.

A night in May, the Bull was on a spree
up in the sky, the Germans had surrendered,
and Edie Johnson was so good to me,
we talked about Japan, and a long war,

and this made Edie very, very tender.
"Don't just sit there!" she laughed, and pulled me forward.
The radio was singing sweet surrender
as we two clasped and struggled without let.

Ah, Edie, I was new at it, and scared,
but I advanced, your puppy on all fours,
and headlong through that night, though trumpets blared,
we only heard ourselves, the little whispers.

We never met again. Wouldn't you know
our orders were being cut that very dawn
when I, dog-tired, snoring in my bunk,
heard the damn whistle, then the hullabaloo

of sergeants, scuttlebutt, and duffle-bags
dragged across bare wooden floors, the thunk
of army trucks pulled up right to the doors,
and the gates slamming. I had no time to think,

and by the telephone MPs kept the score.
My number never came. Now years between
the health and heartache of so many wars
I wonder what I might have said

if I had gotten through. Dear mentor, cunning one,
your page-boy all messed up, your patience of a saint,
your body like a fragrant loaf of bread,
why do you still gleam, the laser in my head?

I sometimes hope you only think I died
in the Pacific, your consoling dream,
and that you talk about me, bleary-eyed,
at The Finn's Place, outside of Rockingham,
where you still go, where Memory belongs —
but that stuff only happens in old songs.

Ballad of the War Bride

Willie, on leave, got married, and came home
to show his discharge, and show off his bride,
a gangling, giggling girl from Birmingham
without a cent. His mother almost died.

His father came right out and talked expense,
and told them that this wasn't Alabama.
The kids agreed. As if doing penance
they both found jobs, and soon the money came.

His mother grumbled on, as did his father;
they said they couldn't understand her speech.
A girl with yellow hair was too much bother,
and they were sure that she was using bleach.

One day they told him, fever in their eyes,
"Kick in more money, and we'll save for you."
Then it was that Willie, past surprise,
knew what he and his sweetheart had to do.

One morning, trim deportment a pure sham,
they left for work as far as one could tell,
but with train tickets back to Birmingham.
He called his folks en route, and told them to go to hell.

L'Ultima Rinunzia

> One to suffer, one to cause suffering.
> *Guido Gozzano*

My mother wept, her sickness sure;
solace I had none at heart.
For a poem I kept trying,
while my mother lay there dying.
"Son," she called, "leave your art;
bring me water for my cure."

"I shall call the girl," I said,
"for my work is much too dear.
You may talk to her, and pray
until the coming of the day,
but I must be busy here.
Music fills my head."

Then my mother ceased her turning.
With the coming of the dawn
all my verses seemed to dance.
Sun flashed, like a lance,
shearing steeple, roof, and stone,
toward my window burning, burning.

Ballade of the Sad Celebrities

There goes Jane Fonda with her heavy load
of money. She is shimmering up and down
like mountain laurel rippling by the road
in a bright rush of wind. I like her gown,
and the prim face she wears to bear her crown
of cares, ideals, and other cosmic fears.
A ton of money's not a lot of fun;
winners, when they wince, are winsome dears.

And here comes Johnny, bouncy as a toad
across my TV screen. Such is renown
he scarcely needs a surname. He's the goad
to spur me on to bed where I can drown
my tears of envy for all that I don't own.
His quips and quarrels, and his little leers,
come off as boyishness, the cute put-on;
winners, when they wince are winsome dears.

But I must prate no more, not incommode;
I am no tenor, crying like a clown
all the way to the bank. If this is code
it's paradox, which is no common noun,
but a high dresser, always on the town.
Fame is performing, fears and leers and tears,
and showmanship's the thing, the lovely one:
winners, when they wince, are winsome dears.

Dear Jane, dear Johnny, I am still alone;
you try your best, but you are not my peers,

though I wish, like you, I could finesse a frown.
Winners, when they wince, are winsome dears.

Rewriting the Cagney and Lacey Show

Tyne Daly, how I love you! Where'd you get
that broad Queens accent, and those flaring eyes?
Your quiet smile, it puts me in a fret;
and you're my cousin Josie in disguise?

Of all the hard-boiled girls, and pretty too,
that ever rode Bus 68 at five —
there goes another day — tell me, are you
the one whose stupid brother gave her jive

about becoming an old maid, the one
who wanted his shirt ironed every time
you sat down to do your nails? Did we have bun
once, at some wedding, dancing on a dime?

What a fine topic, Tyne, you are, my theme,
my blooming, bumptious, sharp-tongued TV ghost.
You summon up my past, the streets of Queens,
and Time, the unexpected, welcome guest.

You bring the fantasies, not my cold beer:
the law and order thing, and love on show,
the family, the husband, children near,
and your cop-friend, another woman too.

I bask in the cheap moonlight of the screen,
remembering the girl I never met,
the one who's missing from your cozy scene,
gun put away, and mama baking bread.

I think how nice the world was meant to be
a hundred years ago, on Northern Boulevard.
Her name was Carmen, and she looked at me
across the girl's fence in the old school-yard.

A small boy running past me tossed a note,
a crumpled wad that, opened, simply read,
"Meet me, 3:30. I have a red coat."
It frightened me, I felt my ears turn red,

but I waited all the same, at my "appointed hour."
How could I know that very afternoon
she would turn sick? Sent home, she found no cure.
Next morning teacher told us she was gone.

Those were the years the sexes played apart.
I barely knew her name, or gave a look.
That's how it went, the fright, the shock, the start.
Time has a thing to give me I still lack.

Ah, Tyne, some nights I'm more than just a fan.
Then I become the ghost, not you, the gust
that riffles in your hair, some bathrobe scene
perhaps, with you and Harvey, nothing lost

of that eye-speech cameras carry well
in all those lights and shadows. I'm the script
you're playing to, us millions of jokers all,
your vast, synaptic web, your velvet crypt

of stitched, unstitched electrons on a grid
that is your galaxy. We blink, and you blink back.
It is the night we read, soft, closed eye-lid
of space on which the capillaries track

their filaments of color, densities
of darkness; blood throbs; buttons flash.
My head's my video, and what it sees
is Carmen, Tyne, but never simple flesh.

What is the relevance of all this jazz?
There's me, in an old house, in a small town
in the Midwest: there's you, dear apparition
on a glass, and there's the arty razzmatazz

of music, dialogue, the counterpoint
of staging interspersed with local ads
in other dramas, a collage of cant.
I'm giddy, but I am not driven mad.

I'm driven back into myself, where you
appear, erect and still, like Memory,
the mothering muse whose stories are all true,
the happy ending like the god's decree.

Another house, another town, the viewer
is fooling with the dial, catches your face
and settles back, and smiles. This much is sure:
and stuff of legends is gathering apace.

In the back-yard dogs whimper, garage-doors
give back the light of stars, the glow of lamps.
This is the peace that memory restores,
a splintered moon that glints in hollow stumps
where water settled when the rains came down.
It's water deep enough for dreams to drown,
and in the house the TV roars and roars.

Some Mentors

1. To Answer Robert Frost

(for Spencer Brown)

> The question that he frames in all but words
> is what to make of a diminished thing.

Some things are best unsaid, and best unheard;
not every tattle-tale's a pretty bird,
but here's one now, that cardinal again.
He must proclaim himself. There are no flowers,
the land is bare, but he makes up for ten,
say cardinal flowers from the summer past.
The weather's threatening; we've had snow-showers,
and biting wind in heavy overcast.
The radio keeps bragging about the fall
in temperature; he won't shut up at all.
He may be saying this is for the birds,
and he's an omen. Furies liked to sing.
He may be telling us in his own words,
"If Rage is all that's left, Rage is a pleasant thing."

2. *Cheering Amy Lowell On: "Some Imagist Poems, 1915"*

An editor once put her picture in
the paper. Read the caption: because she
was a grand lady, and by no means thin,
he wrote down, "Amy Lowell and Company."
That brought some laughs and chuckles. As for me,
I still remember being called "Cross-Eyes"
when I was small. Grew out of that, grew wise;
I'm on the lookout now for courtesy.

Lord save us from the likes of Ezra Pound
who made a nasty pun out of her name
because of a book. A matter of some fame,
she faced him down, and took part of his ground,
because, though lacking graces, she had grit,
and like her money, used it, used it, used it.

3. Taking Sides with John Ciardi

    — some words on minus-American poetry

When Robert Lowell hyphenated you —
Italian, hyphen sign, American —
to praise your poetry, your answer ran
in rough-house expletives. Your passion flew,
and subsequently in an interview
you squelched his harmless seeming little hyphen
as not the way to write out citizen.
How culture-vultures smiled at the to-do.

If this is poetry, as may be true,
it's also punctuation, not too thin
a point or line for morals that you drew.
We all know grammar can stick like a pin,
and those who think my point is overdrawn,
they are no friends of yours, nor of mine, John.

Driving East, Thinking of Frank O'Hara

> You don't refuse to breathe do you
> *Frank O'Hara*

You're gone now
from the chummy New York you got used to,
Frank —
you don't know the Museum of Modern Art
is still going begging,
the city is broke,
the parks are being abandoned to the Vandals.
Where did you pick up your lingo, so frou-frou,
so in,
like the palaver a lover might send
in a night letter,
full of outrageous code words?
They're mostly chat, your poems,
it is that simple,
and maybe the strap-hanger humming to himself
in the subway under the river
is what they make up,
the fantasies of a reasonable optimist
on a clammy Friday night,
the end of a busy week.

They're not that simple.
They remind me of Jackson Pollock,
whom I don't care for
as I care for you.
I always wish that Pollock had painted words
to accompany his long arm drips and scrawls

with a handy caption.
We know why you liked him so much:
you wrote the way he painted.
The pavements were your canvas
wherever you strolled tee hee and tsk tsk
gaping at windows,
or glimpsing a headline,
or waving to some pretty someone you didn't know on a bus.

They aren't poems, your poems,
they simply breathe
the way you breathed
the dust and oil-slick of the Queen of Cities,
knowing you had to breathe, or else keep still
for a long time.
They are poems that take a walk—
though not like Prufrock, more like Apollinaire—
as you talk to yourself and your friends,
humming humming and humming
between the snatches of conversation,
and letting the words spill richly, just like paint,
all over your cozy dominion
of street and lobby, luncheonette and bookstore.

You are my favorite action-painter, Frank:
I can always follow the gist of your conversation.
Now you are gone.
Whenever I get back to New York I keep looking
for all the droll beauties you mention,
the mere and the great,
including the possibilities of Khrushchev,
hoping, the same as you,
the day is the right day.

On a Remark by the Poet, Dana Gioia, on Translating

> Translation is inevitable, in the first place,
> because of the curse of Babel ...
> *Robert M. Adams*

It is sheer coveting, that much is clear,
of someone else's folly and surprise,
and soothes your secret fever as you peer
into another person's heart, to see
with calm, untroubled eyes,
how things may be and how things may not be.
The act of a voyeur,
you spy a fellow out, and take his lies
for granted, your own motives less than pure.
Then you fix his measure, take a look
in a strange dictionary, and try your luck.

Out of the poem you gingerly extract
the live-coal from the clinker in the grate:
then envy glossed into cunning tact,
the shimmering in your hands. By fits and starts
you ponder, study, weigh, you extricate
from gritty clots the gleaming private parts.
Soon it's like keeping score:
your pencil flails away, moods don't distract,
and the grisly business leaves no trace of gore.
When you are finished, watch him strut and rage;
it isn't you that's crying in the cage.

This will not do for Homer, you've been told,
or Dante. Shakespeare has the best of it
for changing englished Plutarch into gold.
That wasn't alchemy, but outright theft.
No doubt our mother wit
does well enough — though we are all bereft
since Babel's shame —
to strike a phrase cast from our own stronghold,
but you're translating now, so stake your claim —
we're babbling foreigners all, and none the worse
for Bibles put to native prose and verse.

At the Widow Kate's Retirement Banquet

The guest of honor sits, as patient as
the furniture, and listens maybe to our talk
about her service to the cold country
of working for a living forty years,
and raising up three kids without a man.
Among the cataracts of drapes, the cliffs of glass,
she gleams, the slender willow by the stream
of our smooth conversation, the fragile fact.
And old boys joke, and the Big Boss swoops down
from the eagle's nest of his democracy
to grasp her by the hand, and wish her well;
while all she does, like a willow by a stream
in sunlight, is to toss her flowing hair.

Spoiled by All My Tyrants

Spoiled by all my tyrants, and whomped to bed,
but kissed for my blond curls from time to time,
the shoved to school like the bound refugee
Authority had asked for, all my brothers
gruff and soon gone growing, to come back
and bring me all the grace of the Green Fair,
I had a precious training, and clean hands.
On the cold bench my mother creaked her grief
to understand my words; the school salute
I pressed upon the flag could only scare her.
On my dark kind, why have you left me bleating,
to learn trite courtesies and lowland ways,
when all I wanted was my rightful place
as the last son beside my father's table?
Tell him that as I grow my hair turns darker.

The Marionettes

See how they dream their wooden dreams,
pine legends in their painted eyes.
Their ardor is of crepe and chalk;
the fire is their only surprise.

Catch how they mouth their gargoyle talk;
they even love with a scratching sound.
The fire is their only surprise,
Pinocchio burning himself to the ground.

Watch how they dance their clacking dance;
their kiss is like the breaking of a box.
They would sprout leaves, like fingers of sense —
Master Gepetto, how they dance,

sauntering past with chirping knees
through the proscenium's feast of eyes.
Wanting not to made of wood,
the fire is their only surprise.

City of iron metaphors,
your children applaud their angular pranks
as their freak noses bump in fiction.
Do they hope that mothers will offer thanks?

See how they turn their necks of bark,
wound and wired for noise and friction.
They are not children lost in the dark.
the fire is their only surprise.

Friend Cricket, like a piccolo,
you weep from the wall of your prophecy:
they are so lonely racked on the shelves;
they can weep splinters if only they try.

They're not content to be themselves,
but plot a vegetable sovereignty,
with their sinister, sonorous Italian names
dreaming some varnished mythology.

The fire is their only surprise.
They court the green and yellow courtesan;
in her silver dress she is telling them lies.
The moon is their favorite citizen.

And all the unsteadied by their pilgrimage
to this last boondock of a grimy town.
visited by their pushcart prompt parades
I spy a hundred wooden strangers in the lemon dawn.

They are shouting I love you in an old dialect,
their chatterbox tarantellas waking the glades—
Columbina, the barking of Melampo,
the toy apples of Giuseppina's breasts,

shimmering forth from the ultimate shores of illusion,
Puncinello, staring with eyes of pearl,
singing I love the child with the blue hair,
I love the green and yellow girl.

II.

The Bocce Court on Lewis Avenue

The Bocce Court on Lewis Avenue

The poem that follows is, I guess, a praise-song for the old neighborhood where I grew up. I think poetry started as praise and supplication, and celebrated triumphs, defeats, weddings, and Deity. I believe all poets, at some time or other in their creative lives, feel a strong nostalgia for the legendary beginnings of their craft, and I have to own up to it here, I have yielded to the engrossing temptations of such feelings, and tried to be a bard. For those readers who would like to ponder this concept further, I can offer no better suggestion than an engagement with Mary Renault's biographical novel, *The Praise Singer*, where she imagines with flair and scholarship the life of Simonides, (6th century B.C.), an ancient poet who followed Homer.

Corona, scene of the action of my poem was in my childhood and old, neat, dowdy, peaceful section of Queens, a borough of New York City which used to be called in those days "the borough of small homes." (Its main claim to fame today is as the home of the New York Mets baseball team, Shea Stadium.) To give one an incisive idea of the stakes involved in the "war" between Mayor Lindsey (1970) and Corona Heights, one need only reflect chastely that $45,000 homes were being condemned by New York City at a surrender price of $21,000.

The struggle of these few people over a no longer unimportant tract of land bounded by a dump, vast car junk-yards, and the busy IRT subway system, attracted national attention—much joking by TV reporters especially—and vociferous support of celebrities such as Norman Mailer and Jimmy Breslin. The four-year war was a heroic story, and deserves a poem.

I close with an excerpt from the New York Times that describes, in cold detail, the capitulation of the Mighty to the wrath of the people:

From a *New York Times* story, December 3, 1970 —

New Corona Plan
Spares 59 Homes

City to return 31, move 28
in Compromise on School

Fifty-one homeowners in Corona, Queens, who had fought vainly for three years against displacement for a proposed high school, won an extraordinary last-minute reprieve yesterday at City Hall.

The City, which already had taken title to their homes in a fight most people thought was over, offered to return the property of 31 owners and to move the small frame and cinderblock houses of 28 others to new sites a block away.

The compromise was described as the first time in which the city had ever offered to return a large tract of property taken in eminent domain....

The Bocce Court on Lewis Avenue

—*New York Times* photograph, December 2, 1970, by Barton Silverman

1. The center of the shot

That man caught in the center of the shot—
right arm thrust forward, shoulder jutting out—
is shooting, has released his bocce ball
with line-drive fury, cunning underhand
at his opponent's ball close to the ball—
the tiny one—that gives the winning point.
The trick is to put spin into his throw
so that the flung ball arcs into its target
and grinds on contact with the enemy
and knocks it clean away, yet stays in place it
itself, snug-dug into the dirt. You call that English,
which is pool-player's jargon good enough
for any old Italian playing bocce.
The ball is coming at you with great speed.
A good displacement makes a popping sound
of wood on wood, like a revolver-shot,
and this is what the word *sparata* means,
the word spectators cry if the ball hits.
Displacement is the dearest thing in bocce;
not dump-shot, not home run, it can reverse a point,
turn losers into winners. This leads to drinking.
Here, as displacement, it is kinder than
the one the mayor plans, our suave John Lindsay
who has ordered the demolition of this street,
this bocce court four generations old,
to make room for a high school playing-field.

2. The left border of the photograph

Look at the beefy man in the business suit
loitering at the edge of the photograph
behind the low plank fence that frames the court.
He's a little shifty. He has no business there.
He should be on the job. He stole away
more like a burglar than the banking man
he is in real life. He's the mortgage-man
at the Corona Savings Bank, the one
these bocce players save at, up the block.
He's glancing at his wrist watch, but that's sham,
and not his conscience; he has time enough.
His paperwork is all tied up — no deals;
the whole town is agog with condemnation,
the talk of lawyers' notices, and rumor
is funning through the streets like a cold wind.
But what the hell, he thinks, time on his hands;
the game's a hot one: he'll just bum a drink,
and maybe place a bet.

The Jug of wine is set
beneath the bench those men are sitting on
at the court's far end. They face the camera,
they watch the game, conversing in low tones.
In front of the, of course, and in the way
the mailman stands — not the insignia
on his left solder — weaving from side to side
and tilting over in anxiety
because the ball just thrown is headed for
his point-ball. He's the opponent of the man
who flung the ball straight at the camera.

The Dance at St. Gabriel's — 305 — Felix Stefanile

He's almost dancing now, and doubled over,
wishing up a jinx of pure distraction;
you'd think that he was dodging someone's aim —
he is; he doesn't want to be displaced.
His fist are clenched; the frown upon his face
is fierce enough to scare the little boy
whom you can't see, behind the privet hedge
that forms the border of the photograph.
The boy is squatting, hiding from the man
who threw the ball, his father. He'd been told
at least five minutes past to scoot back home
and pick up some cigars. The innocent fact
is that he cannot tear himself away.
He is afraid that if he goes away
his father, his strong father, will not win.
He too is wishing you a mighty jinx,
his fingers crossed against the tilting mailman.
Of course the whole town's wishing up a jinx
to topple City Hall, and save the homes.

3. *The right border of the photograph*

The ball's still in the air. This poem has wings.
Those three men to the right of your frozen state,
almost outside the frame, each with one foot
perched on the sacrosanct old plank
that separates them from the bocce game
(they look as though they want to jump inside)
are the Greek chorus here. They may not know that.
They're young, and off from work, or between jobs.
You stand around a lot in Corona Heights:
it's easy — there's the coffee shop, the park,
an ice cream parlor with Italian ices,
and Leo's Pizzeria. There's this game.

One fellow, eyes intent upon the ball,
is muttering out of one side of his mouth
to the fellow next to him. You hear it all.
"We should all go on strike, my mother said.
I said to her, Ma! Go on strike, what strike?
How can I go on strike if I ain't working?"
The others laugh. Now the three shift
in unison, as to cue, from turn
to counter-turn; they're following the ball.
They murmur; things are coming up Act Five.
At that same moment the small cameraman
inside your head is wondering to himself
if this will be the shot that gets the page.
In this seedy part of Queens, where no one goes
unless it's home, the machinery is in place
to bring the ball down, like a god, with wings.

4. *Foreground*

Yes, you are hearing something; that's a voice
you hear. Those women chattering aren't in the picture,
but have just met a few feet from the court
on the cracked sidewalk. Now they stop to talk
about the story in the *Daily News*,
the one describing once again their anger,
the tactics they have used to show resistance
to progress, as the politicians call it—
the worry for their homes, the neighborhood,
their frugal habits, simple histories,
and the surprising sensible suggestion
that Jimmy Breslin offered, in a column,
that maybe all the old homes could be moved,
and not demolished. It is a last hoe.
The middle-aged woman, celery sticking out

of her shopping bag, an inch below her nose,
is fuming. As she shakes her head the greens
tremble their little flags, and her voice rises:
"The lawyer from the City said to me
that we could put my mother in a home
after we left. He could arrange for it.
I said to him, I said, I'll scrub floors first.
That's not the way we treat our people here."
The younger woman swings her handbag up
to point a finger at the cameraman:
another foot and she could smack him square
in the head with it. "I told that man to come
and see my fig tree, take a picture maybe.
The one my father planted. I told him,
these are my memories, this house, that tree.
How do you pay for memories, I said."

5. The frame to hold the photograph

Behind the scene the mayor's playing ball —
that bocce ball's his stone of Sisyphus —
with the local politicians just as quick
if not as slick as he is, not as pretty.
The struggle of the homes is out of hand:
old women and children chanting, homemade posters
nailed to the telephone poles, the TV clip
of a moustachioed codger standing by
a bulldozer and aiming his old shotgun.
The gaggle of reporters is shocked and pleased
to find their startling feature a few blocks
from the IRT, in rowdy-dowdy Queens.
The Mayor contemplates a walking tour
of Lewis Avenue in his shirt sleeves
the way he did in Harlem, where it worked.

No, Cary Grant, you'll shed more than a crease
if you do that, and meet up with these people.
They'll greet you with their ancient imprecations,
oaths of ancestors, feats of profanity
admired even by some poets and scholars,
like, say, Henri Michaux, who in hushed lines
once spoke in awe of "Neapolitan calumny,"
the kind to make a man drop dead in shame.
Your mayoral campaign has hit the skids;
one thing sure—you'll not be re-elected.
The Boards of Estimate, of City Planning,
of Education, a huge over-world
of bureaucrats and condemnation lawyers
(like Cuomo), precinct captains, the gauleiters
of the two major parties have sniffed the wind
of national as well as local rumor.
To use the old cliché, they are all laughing stock
for both comedians and columnists.
Laughter is not their business; money is;
this is a gang that has to save its ass.

Read, in snatches, their statement to the press—
... deplores the tactics... three and a half years...
of hardship for the 69 families...
must not occur again... delay and anguish....
deputy mayor (Lindsay will not be quoted)
denies duplicity... Corona Heights
is maimed, but saved, some houses moved, five demolished.
The Battle of Bad Acres has been won
by a few angry people, and a fig tree.

6. Blast of music

At Leo's Pizzeria *Vo-Lah-re's* playing
on the machine that lights up like a steamboat.
The guys and gals are watching the TV
that's turned down low, Gabe Pressman on the screen.
One fellow, coming out of the Men's Room,
bursts into tremolo, *nel blu dipinto di blu*...
as the bartender, telling him to shut up,
darts out to the nickelodeon, pulls the cord,
stands splay-footed, eyes riveted to the screen
Suddenly Gabe Pressman fills the place;
his soothing voice drifts over the dark room,
almost a homily, and gives the news,
the statement. Names are named. They lift wolf cries,
pound the bar and punch up on each other,
grins on their faces. Now the bartender
re-plugs the nickelodeon, and darts back
to hustle drinks, and when the music blares
they sing along. Gabe Pressman stares and stares.

7. Center

Back at the bocce court the photograph
is hatching in the black and silver box.
Tomorrow, like a swooping bird, the ball
the old man flung will spread across the pages
of the *New York Times,* and all the other papers.
The little boy who disobeyed his father
is standing now. Squatting was no fun.
His eyes are wide and darting; he wrings his hands
an instant, and then gives a hesitant clap,
quivering as he tries to skip and jump,
yet not be noticed. Now his blushing face

is round O his lips make crying out.
He feels his heart careening, plunging down
with the plunging ball. Ah, that colliding crack
of wood on wood as loud as demolition,
sparata: the shot heard around City Hall.
He whirls into a dance, then checks himself.
the way he races home now you would think
he thinks he bears a message from the gods.
Behind him a voice shouts, "It's on the News..."
He takes it for the wind that speeds him on.

III.

Geographies

… not the object described, but the light that falls on it,
like the lamp for a distant room.
Boris Pasternak

The Old Clothes Tree

Leans in the hall
and wobbles now and then
beneath his pack.
Not what he used to be.

But last night I dreamed
he swirled his cape of laundry
twirled his bent umbrella
dancing in the dark.

This morning
rushing past
I brushed against him.
He flailed his empty sleeves
in a little jig
and tossed his hat
in the air.

Midwest Fantasy

1. Winter: Red's Barbershop

Boys who played the games they've always played,
at nine years old, at forty nine years old,
the snow, the moose, the lake, the air so cold
it hurt to breath, as someone said,
calling to his buddies up ahead —
he slipped into an icy ditch, and spilled
his guts caroming, but his rib-cage held.
He laughed and laughed. His buddies called him mad.

The barbershop is buzzing up a storm
of memories this snow-sharp afternoon, some boys
as full of liquor as they are of noise,
such is the fellowship that keeps them warm.
Later, back home, their women will cut loose
at them about that moose, that bloody stupid moose.

2. Spring: The Mourning Dove

The mourning dove, soft idiot on my sill,
pecks at the glass. Surprised it does not yield
he straightens up, and blinks his button eye,
and like a small parade struts back and forth,
then shows his white behind and flies away.

3. *Summer: August*

This heavy hour,
this ton of light;
the blinding pane,
all I can do is squint

At the garden with its look
of frost in early dawn,
where a cricket is making music.
The mirage cuts like a knife.

Then I stare as hard as I can
at the squirrel in the pawpaw branch
not three feet from the window.
He is heaving, heaving.

I think of the flameshapes of the corn,
tumescent and gold,
that point and point.
Where my dream walks they cackle.

4. Autumn: Indiana

Now the sheaves crackle
to the touch, like new dollar bills.
Glowing October. The irrigation pond
shimmers.

Like a stampede the stand of trees
in the distance shudders its green mane —
glint and ripple of shadow,
Mist on the ground running silver.

The ditch by the road heaves with plumes.
A rock shows its head among the yarrow.
Poetry is a gun
aimed at the fat hare trundling across

the field. He comes to a stop,
sits up, ears twitching.
I have been at my window all morning,
my page covered with the showering thresher's dust
that flirts in the breeze like gauze,
like a flag.

The Hunters

The hunters from the city, strictly dressed
in store-bought reds and yellows, trailing smells
of shaving lotion, board the country train.
With pale and jolly looks they settle down
in the far corner, weapons clattering
in small, efficient shocks, start playing cards
slapped on an old valise across their knees.
They've come to rent our poor and shaggy county;
they sprawl in corduroy poses, noisily,
while lower on the skyline, the sun setting
chips over river into scales and whorls
that float downstream, like scattered, golden feathers.

On Painting a Bike

The weather, like a tourist here before,
returns in patch and plaid to lawn and tree;
three robins repossess the courteous shore
of our brick lake, and scold the continent.
The children's bicycles are blue this year;
I wonder now what last year's colors meant.

In my own childhood, when the weather came,
April or May, I felt a busy need
to be at painting—it was like a game
of changing all the furniture of the earth,
made up of bikes and wagons it would seem;
I brushed away for all that I was worth.

I took such satisfaction in my stain
I caused the garden in the back to glow,
and those old irons glimmered in the rain
like famous weapons fabulous to win.
Mine was a landscape painted over then
might make a proper serpent change his skin.

Now I'm turning gray; the season's green;
there's not a single fault that I can dye.
Some kids ride past, each eager to be seen,
with arms outspread, like wings, as after all
I did myself once, til I had a spill
that skinned me red as Eden in the fall.

From an Apartment House Window

Outside, the cars sleep peacefully, like sheep
huddled in asphalt valleys. Over all,
the moon, imagined shepherd, seems to creep
by yard and building, and by sagging wall,
a quiet figure in a field of brick.
There is a stillness here would surely suit
Theocritus, more than my rhetoric
that dreams these stones would ring to hear his flute.

Binary Rhymes

What are the generations of the fly?
The logarithms of astronomy

can measure them in all their magnitude,
compute the leaves that populate a wood.

Numbers, numbers, are the current rage.
Are the sands beyond number beyond reach?

With metaphysical machines that count
piano-rolls of algebraic cant

we manufacture meanings where there was
mere wordless music, dunes, shaggy grass.

O lovely lotteries, o chips and chance!
It is for principle I stay a dunce.

Irises

Time's lackey, but the lord of sun this day,
I watch the garden from my window, glance
at the green rubble rusting in the clay
of my new-city suburb, note the pert
irises at their posture by the fence,
resembling cardboard figures stuck in dirt.

Concordance and construction in their sure
trim rods, from which the leaves, like blades,
work on the wind the menace of their humor,
I marvel that their flags now fly so limp.
In all the brick and hazard of these shades
the sun had lent his legendary lamp

and shone, a Hero, who was not. They stand,
plumage awry now, swords askew, like troops
at ease in a parade form Bogus Land
where generals led the armies down wrong streets;
they crack in wind like locusts, like all hopes
faltered in alternating hails and heats.

Where is my sin of cynicism here?
I am no long fellow, with words of worth,
to argue celebration at a bier,
when, for a week perhaps, they get their wish
before they tumble once again to earth,
the blonde and tousled head, the ragged flesh.

The Insect World

Poised paradox, whose slender, clever claws
resemble, maybe, hands that clasp in prayer,
artfully scythed to sweep a struggling spouse
young to your breast, while his legs thrash the air
in frantic waltz, his flesh your wedding feast,
nomenclature's humor suits you least.
Grass window, yours is grief I do not share.

Monsters of childhood glimmer form your face,
amaze the singing meadow. Robots stalk
near rose and garden hedge, by Queen Anne's lace,
tumbling the simple buggers for a lunch.
Insect, or pious preacher, little hawk,
serving up sermons, all you say is Crunch.

The Motel at the End of the Ramp

Our hamburgers ooze like the blob
from outer space. We are all tired
and trivial. We are eager pioneers
believing that whatever it is we do
it is best to get there in a tremendous hurry —
buns through a car window, and the plastic cups
rolling in the wind on the asphalt
of the American dream. We are young;
we are old and overfed, in Hawaiian shirts.
Our children are smeared with ketchup like blood.
Here then, Thomas Jefferson, is your miracle.

Our roads all lead to roam another horizon,
suburbs attached to them like barnacles;
in the dangerous wash of our wealth
the hills soar and dive like sounding whales.
Why poetry? What glamors here is the motel
at the end of the ramp, lit up like the Titanic,
before the great iceberg of history.
People are zooming in, and zooming out,
young couples, families, the well-dressed terrorists.
I doze to good old Mancini on the Muzak;
I sleep to a whine of trucks, and god-loud thunder.

Andrew

Friend, heavy survivor,
you bear the bull's lowered brow,
ready for comers.

To look at you is to understand
jungles are not nice.
My mind creates tableaux

set behind glass — don't touch —
in memory's museum,
especially one of a classroom

and teacher calling you wop.
Or that night in Linden Park
when, head lowered,

you told me your mother was dead.
We were fourteen,
completely uncomforted.

I suppose things are better today.
We are offered courses on dying.
The joggers tell us, Love yourself.

Old puff-belly baldhead,
you listen to your kids complain,
and smile.

You make a killing at the track
and zoom home in your huge car,
full of frowns.

For you a proverb might be set:
do not thank the gods too loudly,
or they will hear you and change their minds.

Brother, fellow loser,
I know why in these enlightened times
you still tend the Sacred Heart

on the wall
outside your bedroom
with fragrant candles:

it is the one trophy you understand,
as Jesus taught—
we are all nailed to the wall.

The Metaphysics of Winter

Here is a stone whose rugged round
on this November afternoon
glows from the center of its mound
of leaves, and looks just like the moon.
It is not smooth, but hard and bright,
as what will happen pretty soon,
when the green garden changes light
and what shines bright will shine like bone.
Then sun and moon, pure incident,
like Cain and Abel where they went
will daze and dazzle earth turned stone,
like the first skull of Testament.

Two Translations

UMBERTO SABA: *Ulysses*

When I was young I sailed the Dalmatian coast.
Great islands bloomed on the wave; above them flew
once in a while a bird in search of prey.
Covered with kelp, and slippery, under the sun
they shone as beautiful as emeralds.
When night came, and in the high tide they vanished,
with our sails underwind we ducked for the deep
to flee that perilous snare. Today, like that,
my kingdom is No Man's Land. My harbor
burns lanterns for foreigners, and I turn back to sea,
pressed ever on by my unbeaten spirit,
and by my broken-hearted love of life.

UMBERTO SABA: *The Boy and the Shrike*

A boy became enamored of a shrike.
It was a novelty of what he heard
a hunter say about that marvellous bird:
how many vows he made to own a shrike!

He got one, and forgot her, just like that.
Poor bird, strung up inside her window-cage,
she mourned alone in silence for the sky
far off, and irretrievable to her sight.

He only thought of her a certain day
when, out of boredom, or some kind of spite,
he clenched her in his first, and felt a pain.
She bit him, and flew off. And since that day,

and for that hurt, he loves her all in vain.

Elegy, 1942

Fort Devens, Massachusetts

Dowd was the old man of the company,
the one we listened to. He taught us tricks,
like sewing, or he showed us how to roll
a cigarette, or how to take stove black
and cover over cracks in a worn locker
and make it shine. Whenever he got drunk
he'd sing, in a low whisper, some old tune,
"An Orphan and in love," and go to sleep.
He cowed those blackjack players in the back
who liked to stay up late, and swear and smoke,
and keep us all awake, night after night.
When Dowd was by, we slept like innocents.

He heard Cerruti swearing once, and ribbed him,
told him that was some prayer the seminary
was teaching all the boys. Cerruti blinked,
and kept on blinking, searching for the words.
"That seminary is none of your business."
We all knew that Cerruti had washed out
of the seminary, and gone home. In shame
he left home then—imagine—for the Army.
Big Dowd leaned over him, grinned, shook his head:
"It's guys like me who swear. We don't know words.
That leaves holes in the head we paper over

with swear-words. You have learning. You should read,
and study things, not try to be like us."
He walked away. Cerruti blinked again,
and lowered his head to buff his combat boots.

Dowd was shipped out. It was for convoy duty,
an anti-aircraft crew. His empty cot
was taken over soon by someone else,
and that was that. We all forgot about him
except Cerruti; they kept in touch with cards,
and then the cards stopped coming. Came a day,
months later, Nally told us Dowd got his
in the North Sea. The whole convoy went down.

Cerruti dropped his boots, and walked outside;
I watched him through the window, pacing, blinking,
kicking at gravel, searching for the words,
until like death-besotted Lear he shouted
fuck it fuck it fuck it fuck it fuck it.

Hubie

> Army experiments with mixed units:
> Negroes being admitted into white
> companies.—
> *News Item, 1943*

You, Hubie, were the one and only black
in our whole crazy outfit. You had a knack
for fending off out clumsy comradeship.
You were a ferret at a Freudian slip
or condescension: (Let's ask Hubie, too?)
You always answered, "Cut it out, will you?"
Except one time: the night we made to go
to the Anselmo Club, and wouldn't you know,
we challenged you, we forced you, kidnapped you
to come along. You came. We wrecked the place.
The frightened 4F doorman mentioned race,
held his hand up to his pasty face,
and said you had no card, no "membership,"
He tried to close the door; Paul knocked his grip,
and hollered, "He's our guest!" Then the poor guy said No,
and Paul, half drunk already, just let go.
That was a fight we all enjoyed but you;
the cops came, and your black skin saved our hides,
because the owner blamelessly denied
that there was trouble, and we made no news.
No news was good for him, and good for us,
but the drink you drank that night was bitter, bitter juice.

Then there was Captain Jones from Millidgeville
(GEE-AY!) who hated you so hard it killed
to hear him give you his Boy-this, Boy-that.
He hated all of us, but that was pure so what
to the dockside bruisers, city toughs,
and all the ill-sorted country roughs
that made up our sad clan of prison-chasers:
we knew that you were the true King of Losers.
Maybe that's why we liked you, let that stay,
from ignorance to shame to light of day.
Jones ran us like a chain-gang, that's for sure,
but your bland moon-face shone, "Endure, endure."

Once I glimpsed you with the Enemies.
It was their singing time. They were a breeze
to guard, no trouble. It was a heavy night
of stars and blooms, of shadows that turned bright.
A kid cupped his right hand up to his face
the way they did to magnify the voice,
and winked at you. Hubie, you winked back.
It was a sign between you for a song,
and then he gave their yodel, loud and long,
fronni e limoni; which maybe signified
some legend lost when ancient glory died,
but left its echo. No one would begin
before the signal, *lemon leaves*, had run
in gross annunciation. The same phrase
would introduce each stanza. In a daze
I heard the eerie music, though this time

the voice I heard was yours, in Neapolitan rhyme,
and my translation of it here is a crime:

Oh leaves of the lemon tress! It's in the shape of crosses
they are constructed, all the gates of prison,
the better to destroy the sons of mothers.
Ah, Hubie, what a maundering in my heart
to hear you go falsetto sob and start,
and grace-note that muezzin-vaunt of words,
gliding the vowels over, like slow birds,
the drawn out line, I thought my head would burst.
For their lament those lads made you sing first;
you knew the chant; it could have been the blues,
three lines of heartbreak, blood down to your shoes.
Then came the answers, in the same old notes,
one fellow, then another, golden throats—
tears for a mother, or a girl back home,
some nasty verse on the Pope in Rome,
and when your turn came round again you sang
about the way the bells of Nola rang.
Mad Captain Jones's "damn eye-talian crew"
had caught your grave compassion trusted you,
and taught you more Italian for a song
than the rest of us had learned the whole year long.
Those distant bells, they did you no more good,
that did the chimes of elegant Englewood,
New Jersey, where you came from, preacher's son,
out of a tiny Baptist congregation
made up of cooks and gardeners, garbage men,
and other service people all hemmed in.

The war came, you were ready, just like me,
which meant no job, no future, and no money.

What now comes back to me, old Hubie, is
how you and I could sit and shoot the breeze
those Sunday afternoons, when things went dead
in repple-depple camp. The peace went to my head.
We chuckled about week-end roll-calls, played
the same each muster: mostly, no one up
except us cowards who were thin on hope,
afraid to miss the check and rate KP,
although in truth half our company
slept through. The guys took turn as stand-ins, one
for every two or three in mock attention,
answering for O'Toole or Policetti
or Garbatino, Sergeant Parmelee
stared straight down at his pad, and called the lot,
then swung around to go back to his cot.
"Why don't you slack off, Hubie?" I asked once.
You snorted, as though you took me for a dunce,
patted my knee with that ham hand of yours,
and said, "Because for me it would just be my arse.
With my complexion can't you see the fun?"
The simple truth fell on me like a ton.

Poor twins, we were dispatched on the same day,
a lot to do, pick up our pay,
strip down our cots—"They might just change their minds,"
our sergeant snarled, "so move your fat behinds" —
sweep out the years, go listen to the lecture

The Dance at St. Gabriel's — 336 — Felix Stefanile

on Re-enlistment and Reserve, some double feature;
then scoot to chow, and back to Camp Supply.

The Quartermaster goof-off, Sleepy Eye,
just brushed our gear aside, and made us sign.
On our way out we passed a clothing bin;
talk about brave! I knew we were civilians
when I snitched a cap, an Eisenhower jacket,
and so did you, you bum, and you said, "Fuck it!"
The whole platoon was gone when we got back,
the silence of the barracks pure whip-crack
of memories in my head, I stared at you.
You said, "There's still one thing for us to do,"
and handed me a sheet, hodge-podge
of name address, and Bible verse for pledge
all loyalty, no betrayal. To make things worse
I read aloud that thundering, crying verse
because you told me once I was a poet.
What boobs we were; how kind we didn't know it.
I handed you a map of streets, instructions,
accompanied by four-letters imprecations
of what would happen if you didn't write me,
or come and visit. Then you'd have to fight me.
The map showed names of streets and bus route numbers.
All at once we stopped. We were stuck dumb.
You blinked your eyes, and made a choking noise.
That was enough for me; I lost my voice.

We neither of us wrote. What came
between? It was not a forgetting. It was time

that took its aim, and brought us down like fools.
We had survived—according to the rules—
the deaths, the separations and all the cant
of war, of honor, and the special rant
of patriotism. We had saved our skins
through years of soldiering, the tightrope dance
of danger, boredom whatever we fought for;
ourselves, we knew, were the true spoils of war.
We moved from that into the orgy of
the personal release of pre self-love.

The time is gone for what we should have said
or done, old Hubie. All the dead are dead.
Time was once ripe. Now time's a rotten thought.
Yet blow me down, and scratch me for an ought,
we buddied to the end, just to endure.
(There is a thought here that is less than pure.)

A black man and a white man, that's for sure,
this other war, and the cagey cowardice
of habit, turning honest blood to ice.
I think that we were brothers once, "The Twins,"
the fellows called us, making their wide grins.
What's left is poetry, the penance for my sins.

Honorable Army Discharge

My heart was full of money, and my head
was full of dreams, the day that I got home
for good. My mother cried and cried, my sisters
cried; my brother, turned fourteen, just stared
and laughed, and stuck his finger to his head
and rolled his eyes. It was as if to say
that things were back to normal now, and crazy.

When Pop came home from work, harroomph, harroomph,
he asked me if I'd been to see my room,
the new paint job. He tripped upon a word,
said something about a new bloom sweeping clean.

That broke things up we laughed, we all sat down
to eat and talk. I choked the pasta down
as best I could; it was so rich and sweet,
the taste of a largesse I had forgotten.
I never guessed at yearning, those lost years,
until late in the night. The new paint job
seared through my nostrils, and brought out the tears,
my room so small, so safe, so quiet I heard
the drumming in my ears, my heart's own cannon
time and again go whoosh and whoosh and thud.

The Veteran

Four hundred poems ago
my time off was a conspiracy
to undermine the Muse's citadel;
I worked bombs at my desk.

Now thoughts of winding down by noon-time,
my beer like a bubble bath…

thoughts of the sunny garden,
that new book on ancient Greece,
and our tilted sundial casting its shadow
towards the grackles, who don't care.

Unbudgeable, and full of light,
the hollow hackberry stump by the fence
grins like a mouth;
there are vines at the base trailing upward.
For a moment I recall
the trappings of Dionysus,
the god in the tree.

Nobody has to tell me
poems are of the earth,
craft trains the vine.

For that reason I keep worry away
in a doze, in a dream
of Apollonian summer;
my torch doused in the sun.

In a city as out of date
as Edna St. Vincent Millay
a young poet once burned his candle at both ends,
and starved himself for a book.

Look at him now, smiling,
paunch-happy
like that old Tabby, no leopard cub,
sniffing at the tree stump
before him.
The poet's wife, no maenad,
brings him another beer.
Famed be damned.

THE COUNTRY OF ABSENCE

POEMS AND AN ESSAY

FELIX STEFANILE

BORDIGHERA PRESS

Library of Congress Control Number: 2012937242

© 2000 by Felix Stefanile

All rights reserved. Parts of this book may be reprinted only by written permission from the authors, and may not be reproduced for publication in book, magazine, or electronic media of any kind, except in quotations for purposes of literary reviews by critics.

Printed in the United States.
Published by
BORDIGHERA PRESS
John D. Calandra Italian American Institute
25 W. 43rd Street, 17th Floor
New York, NY 10036
VIA Folios 18
ISBN 978-1-59954-045-0

OTHER BOOKS BY FELIX STEFANILE

POETRY
The Dance at St. Gabriel's
In That Far Country
East River Nocturne
A Fig Tree in America
The Patience that Befell
River Full of Craft

TRANSLATIONS
If I Were Fire: 34 Sonnets of Cecco Angiolieri
The Blue Moustache: Some Italian Futurist Poets
Umberta Saba: 31 Poems

ACKNOWLEDGMENTS

The poems listed here first appeared in the following publications, and are gratefully cited:
Approach: "Antonio Stefanile," "Letter from a Friend in Exile"
Differentia: "Farfalla"
Experiment: "Feast of San Gennaro"
Evansville Review: "Emily"
New Letters: "Andrew"
Poetry: "The Marionettes," "A Fig Tree in America," "Atlantis," "Poem for Selma"
Perspective: "Back Home in Indiana"
Poetry Broadside (NY): "How I Changed My Name, Felice"
Quicksilver: "The Day We Danced the Saint"
Sewanee Review: "Ballad of the War Bride"
Whelks Walk Review: "Carmen"

The translation of Umberto Saba's poem, "Ulisse," titled "Ulysses," first appeared in *Umberto Saba: 31 Poems* (Elizabeth Press), permission of Linuccia Saba. The Italian text is from Saba's collection, *Il canzoniere* (Mondadori). The Italian text of the sonnet by Cecco Angioglieri is from *Cecco Angioglieri*, ed. Gigi Cavalli (Rizzoli). The epigraph to Felix Stefanile's poem, "In That Far Country," is from a poem by Selma Stefanile, "I Know a Wise Bird," from *Sparrow Poverty Pamphlet 42*. The author's poem, "In That Far Country," is from his collection of the same title, *Sparrow Poverty Pamphlet 43*. The poems, "The Catch," "Soldiers and Their Girls," "Honorable Army Discharge," and "Taking Sides with John Ciardi" are from *The Dance at St. Gabriel's* (Story Line Press). "The Americanization of the Immigrant," "The Dance at St. Gabriel's," and "Tony" were first published in *From the Margin: Writings in Italian Americana*, eds. A. J. Tamburri et al. (Purdue University Press).

The excerpt from Felix Stefanile's condensed essay originally published in the *New York Times* under the title, "Confessions of an Editor," is gratefully acknowledged.

The excerpt from Felix Stefanile's essay, "American Is Still a Land of Searchers," originally published in the *Christian Science Monitor*, is gratefully acknowledged.

This book is dedicated to the mythmakers:

Aniello, Genoveffa, Francesco, and Selma

Those who live outside themselves live inside the expectations of others.
— La Rochefoucauld, *Maxims*

If every picture I made was about Italian Americans, they'd say, "That's all he can do." I'm trying to stretch.
— Martin Scorsese, *Premiere* (1991)

Robert Penn Warren used to say that a writer should feel about his country the way he feels about his mother: he loves her, but does not approve of all that she thinks and does.
— Walter Sullivan, *Sewanee Review*

The hyphen is the Go-Between.
— Felix Stefanile

TABLE OF CONTENTS

The Allegory of the Hyphen. An Essay	351
The Catch	365
Tony	366
Feast of San Gennaro	369
The Marionettes	370
How I Changed My Name, Felice	372
A Fig Tree in America	373
Who Would Have Thought	374
Farfalla	375
Antonio Stefanile	376
Carmen	377
Andrew	378
The Day We Danced The Saint	380
Atlantis	382
Letter from a Friend in Exile	384
In That Far Country	386
Ulisse, by Umberto Saba	387
Ulysses, by Umberto Saba	388
Cecco Angiolieri	389
Cecco Complains about His Mother's Cure-all	390
On a Remark by the Poet, Dana Gioia, on Translating	391
The Dance at St. Gabriel's	393
Soldiers and Their Girls	394
Ballad of the War Bride	395
Honorable Discharge	396
Back Home in Indiana	397
To Be Frank about It	398
Taking Sides with John Ciardi	399
A Poem for Selma	400
Emily	402
Hubie	405
The Americanization of the Immigrant	411
About the Author	412

THE ALLEGORY OF THE HYPHEN
Felix Stefanile

I

My book, *The Country of Absence,* has a certain intrigue to it. I have chosen the poems — out of a much larger store — from work of mine that appears in previous volumes. The book, however, is not an attempt at a "selected poems" compilation. It is a gathering of some poems of mine, devoted to the Italian American experience, that lie scattered, in past collections among other material. It also contains new poems, and poems like "Farfalla" that are placed between bookcovers here for the first time, though they have been published in magazines. I leave it to the sages of intertextuality, whose fascinating scholarship plays a role in literary studies, to determine if what I now offer is a late bloom, or in its own right, a first book.

On January 22, 1992, my essay, "America Is Still a Land of Searchers," was published as the Opinion Page focus of the *Christian Science Monitor*. It was the first in a series of Opinion Page essays, by various hands, intended to reflect the cultural diversity in the hemisphere. My original title for the piece had been "Discovering Columbus," but that was the year the name Columbus was a dirty word, and the editors changed the heading. Somebody's heart was in the right place in the paper's Boston office, however, for the caption accompanying the new title reads: "A son of Italian immigrants found his own Columbus voyage, seeking the Other in the exploration of poetry." As an abstract this properly interpreted the theme I set forth in my essay.

A key passage of that brief memoir targets my experience during Story Hour, one Friday afternoon in 5B3, when Mr. Aronowitz, a teacher whom we adored, read from the poetry of Henry Wadsworth Longfellow:

> Because of him I cannot forget Longfellow's dark and lovely poem, "The Tide Rises, The Tide Falls." Longfellow's plangent

language throbbed like a gong in my ears. For two or three minutes I let myself be surrounded by language as by a copious spirit, palpable, inescapable, and thrillingly alien. I became aware of how separated from my familiar world of broken English, street talk, and an Italian dialect I didn't always understand, this airy, melodious universe was. I felt as though I was stepping over a line somewhere, into undiscovered country. Loneliness welled up in me almost like homesickness. The aftershock of that reading stayed with me a long time. I had glimpsed the Other, without whom I could not be whole.

That undiscovered country was the country of absence, where my imagination had never been. I conclude the essay with a comparison of myself to Columbus, tracking the wilderness of my own heart, America as language. Longfellow made me a scribbler at ten years old. In a profound sense my moment of conviction, in an elementary school classroom, formed my life as a poet.

II

I emigrated to Newtown High School in September 1933. Two miles from my Italian neighborhood, the school in demographic terms, was a universe apart. A huge stone edifice, a block square, studded with turrets and a tower, and girdled by a tall, wrought iron fence, it was the landmark building of a solid middle-class community. Here you saw no outward traces of the Depression then raging in the country; no empty stores with soaped-over windows, no unemployed men chatting on corners, no garbage-strewn alleys—the result of reduced public service.

This shift in my context was brought forcefully "home" to me during first roll call. The names pelted around me like a cold rain: Ayers, Baynes, Coombes, Doughty, Lord, Morrison, Perkins, and so on. These were tribes of Other America. I wrapped my new-found shyness around me like a cloak against the weather. The sting was all the more pointed because we Italian Americans were a recent influx, caused by a school redistricting plan only put into operation a couple of years before. We were shunted, as a sizable minority, from our familiar jurisdiction, to a massively Anglocentric and Protestant arena. I felt my unlikeness like a blow.

The occasional racial slur I endured, or overheard, I absorbed with the dogged patience of a boy constantly being warned by his elders to be "nice." You must remember that in the Thirties social struggle took place primarily in the labor movement, not in racial identity coalitions. What I felt were the distinctions of class all around me. The tribes of Other America, unlike me, came to school in suits. Their chat, as I eavesdropped in the lunch room from my always "separate" table, was about week-end tennis matches, tea dances, even croquet on the lawn. To an adolescent from my side of the railroad tracks dividing my neighborhood from theirs, these were important concerns.

Fate delivered me from my isolation through a chain of events I could not have foreseen. Towards the close of my first school year the Mayor's office issued a directive to high school officials to devise a city-wide homework assignment for all English grades: it would consist of an essay on fire prevention. The assignment was to be treated as a competition, with winning entries to be selected, and awards to be conferred. In the spring of 1935 the principal's office, through my English teacher, informed me that I was the recipient of first prize for sophomores. *The Newtown X-Ray*, our school paper, dubbed me "the sophomore of the ages."

About a week later an editor of the paper tracked me down during study period in the auditorium. She was a senior, a rank that at my age imposed attention, and asked me to "write something" for the *X-Ray*. In my beleaguered state of mind this was an invitation that had quasi-official overtones. I pleaded inexperience, but she stood her ground, and I agreed to do my best.

The piece I wrote was an appeal to Newtown to join the "national effort" to prevent Walt Whitman's house in Huntington, Long Island, from being sold to a commercial group interested in converting that "hallowed site" into a roadhouse. I gave the name and address of the Defense Fund organized to raise money to outbid the dastardly "moneychangers," and preserve "this shrine of American letters." My prose, in plain truth, was a précis of a story I had read some weeks before in the *New York Times*, but the cry to heaven was mine. To the joy of the *X-Ray*'s editors—and my own embarrassment mixed with pride—my call to arms attracted several donations from outraged parents, teachers, and other defenders of the faith. The school authorities were delighted to forward the money to the Defense Fund. Months later the Whitman home was rescued, and we all took our share of the credit for it in the *X-Ray*.

Such a flurry of excitement did not elevate me to star status at Newtown. That role, among Italian American pupils, was reserved for Joe Spagna, our famed home run hitter on the excellent baseball team the school fielded that year. But it did open some doors for me. The faculty sponsor of the Garretson Scribes, the school's poetry club, so named for a wealthy donor family that maintained the group in high style, with resources for guest lecturers, poetry "soirees," and other cultural affairs, sought me out and asked me to become a member.

My experience in the Garretson Scribes became the high point of my life at Newtown. For the first time, and in a relatively unconfined setting, I had the opportunity to move in a social milieu that reflected Other America. As you can imagine, the organization was filled with Doughtys and Perkinses, and I had to learn to control my shyness among them. I also profited, hearing my poetry discussed by my peers, from the guidance of a gifted mentor. Frances Butterfield, the faculty sponsor, was a poet herself, and an ebullient Muse, a person whom today we would call an activist. Newtown could not hold her, and in time she went on to become a key functionary on the Board of Education, where, among other duties, she directed the New York City annual high school poetry contest and festival, a well-known event that was invariably covered in the newspapers. She loved poetry, and that love and excitement radiated towards the dreamy adolescents in her charge. She made us feel not only privileged, but responsible. She ran the best poetry writing class I have ever come across, and she did not do so—as teachers seem to do today—by telling us how wonderful we were, but how wonderful poetry was.

III

I date my coming of age as a poet to 1950 when, for the first time, work of mine appeared in *Poetry*. Karl Shapiro, then editor of the magazine, accepted two poems. In that post-World War II decade, *Poetry* was the most renowned verse journal in the English-speaking world, and, for poets, the publication towards which all critical scrutiny turned. A first appearance in its pages took on the nature of a debut before the peerage.

I include one of the two poems, "The Marionettes," in *The Country of Absence*. I cite it because the poem was my declaration, before a key segment of the American reading public, of my unlikeness. The author of "The Marionettes" was not the crestfallen lad of seventeen years before who, in Newtown High School, had felt his unlikeness like a blow. It was my hope that the relentless Italian foregrounding and referentiality of the work would bring a new note to the well-established literary theme of the conflict between Art and Life. We may be sure that Oscar Wilde, when offering his witticism about Life imitating Art, did not have my emphasis on Pinocchio, Master Gepetto, Colombina, and "the barking of Melampo" in mind.

I drank from the well of small victories, and was refreshed. Poetry, the continuum that bridged the gap between the opposing poles of my dual nature as an Italian American, became my hyphen. I had celebrated, in a public manner and on my own terms, the marriage of my American North to my Italian South. My sense of self-verification was immense, and spurred me on.

In 1954 Selma and I issued the first number of a verse journal, *Sparrow*. To give the flavor of this Mom-and-Pop grocery-store operation, let me serve an excerpt from an essay of mine, "Confessions of an Editor," that was published in Bill Henderson's Pushcart Press volume, *The Art of Literary Publishing* (1979). It was reprinted, in a 3,000-word condensed version, in the *New York Times Book Review* of February 17, 1980:

> I have never deluded myself as to the importance of *Sparrow*. I have never wanted to compete with Random House or Doubleday. For philosophical reasons I shall go into later I believe such a fanciful contest is absurd to contemplate and foolish to propose. And I have never thought of poetry publishing as an ideological crusade or a revolution. My motivation for entering the field was, in truth, quite personal and selfish. I wanted to live the life of poetry.

This brief outline of my not so sentimental *education sentimentale* as a budding poet would not be complete without some account of "How I changed my name, Felice," which I wrote in 1958. Here, it seems to me, the thesis and antithesis of the hyphen I have striven so mightily to identify in "The Marionettes" behaves much like a metaphor. The synthesis is the line "Felix was American for me." A fitting off-spring of the collision-and-embrace of Italian and American. Is this a poetics of citizenship taking place?

IV

I want to say something about the canon now, a three-dollar word so fashionable among sociologues, ever-piping in our midst, that it is in danger of becoming pure jargon. I shall do so by discussing Emily Dickinson and the Rap poets in the same breath. Emily Dickinson, a powerful literary icon of the latter half of the twentieth century, was the most marginalized poet in American letters. Unlikeness was her fate, despite her impeccable Puritan genealogy as a member of a family prominent and well-connected in the New England society of her time. The Dickinsons were leaders in the local politics of Amherst, a university town with pretensions.

The story of Emily Dickinson, "the nun of Amherst," is too familiar to need elucidation from me. She has captured the American imagination for her mysterious life of seclusion and the taut, electric probing of her tireless spirit that registered its turmoil through poetry. Her popularity—she died in 1886—remains the Consternation of the Correct. The simple truth is that though she wrote close to 1,800 poems only ten saw publication in her lifetime.

Emily Dickinson was not published because she would not write like a lady. According to the "two spheres" dictum of Victorian America the literary worlds of male and female poets were prescribed by the public authority of taste and decorum—which is what the canon is. This authority demanded of women a verse that was genteel, domestic, of limited scope, and as well-behaved as a caged bird. Passion was permitted in the magazines and newspapers only under certain rules; the passion was to be unrequited, or doomed, or, preferably, quelled by moral resistance.

The record is also clear that Emily Dickinson knew editors and poets, enough of them to make a networking MFA graduate of the present day turn green with envy. Had she complied with courteous requests to revise her creative temperament, and shape her work to pass muster in the general taste of the period, she would have been published more widely. She remained, instead, a poet censored by omission. The etiquette of her spry and sly refusals to mend her literary ways—her correspondence with would-be mentors is fascinating reading—unmask not the poet, but the canon that smothered her career.

Today the poems of Emily Dickinson speak to a vast audience, her readership is international and loyal. The authority that silenced her is a dead letter. In her mind-boggling innocence of purpose the poet's fame gives the lie, also, to a reigning shibboleth of our own era, that "Literature is Power." In Emily Dickinson's case literature was powerlessness. I try to give my response to this gorgeous paradox in the poem "Emily," included in *The Country of Absence*.

There are two inferences to be drawn here. The first is that the canon, for all its force, only endures when society obeys it. When, after her death, the poetry of Emily Dickinson began to be issued in a series of cautiously edited volumes, a surprised public reacted favorably—one of the books went into six printings, I believe—and the red-faced canon of Emily Dickinson's despair started its long retreat. In terms of genuine down-to-earth history, the canon is a fiction that is agreed upon. Disagreement kills it.

The second inference is that the literature of powerlessness exists, and always has. The far-flung past is filled with Emily Dickinsons, John Clares, John Keatses, to mention a selected few from the splendid tradition of the English lyric. Other nations can boast the same phenomenon. In Italy, the slender legacy of three sonnets ascribed to a medieval author identified only as *La Compiuta Donzella* (the accomplished maid) incited debate among scholars. No doubt driven by sexist impulses these offer explanations centering around a male author hiding himself behind an assumed anonymity. Other examples could be served.

A century after the verse of Emily Dickinson was first issued in book form, powerlessness, metamorphosed into its own authority, was once more demonstrated in the rise of Rap poetry. The art of a youth culture sprung from the ghetto, its success—now the mighty darling of the music industry—was as unexpected as that of Emily Dickinson, and as prevailing. Its influence on contemporary writing, especially poetry, cannot be denied. It is being offered as a workshop discipline at writer's conferences, always a sure sign of arrival.

Despite obvious differences, the kinship between these two modes of poetry is compelling. Most significantly, each comes to us unbrokered, in no way mediated by the canon. These poets are self-credentialed. Each mode springs from the same source, the inexhaustible mother lode of English lyric, the Common Measure. They are children of the ballad, with its roots reaching down six hundred years. In Emily Dickinson the lore stems more particularly from the hymn, the late, and refined child of the ballad. Yet her craft retains the pristine directness and simplicity—on most occasions—of the older rhythm, the four-and-three beat of the alternating lines, and the abcb rhyme pattern.

Rap, instead, finds itself at home in the "unwritten" tradition of "Sir Patrick Spens" or "The Wife of Usher's Well," with a tendency to be broad in its hints, bold in its humor and anger, and less regardful of the niceties Emily Dickinson is prompt to observe. Rap boasts and swaggers; Emily squeals, and calls a snake *a narrow fellow in the grass*. Both modes, however, visit sorrow and death and love regularly, and with the passion of the anonymous legends of unwritten tradition. In this sense each mode creates, stunningly sometimes, not symbol but myth, the eternal verity practiced over and over. Emily Dickinson's "I dreaded that first Robin so" (348, Johnson), which anticipates T.S. Eliot's opening lines from "The Wasteland" (*April is the cruelest month*), portrays a marauding New England spring with a cinematic sweep of flooding immediacy. I give the first two stanzas:

> I dreaded that first Robin so,
> But He is mastered now,
> I'm some accustomed to Him grown,

> He hurts a little, though —
> I thought if I could only live
> Till His first Shout got by —
> Not all Pianos in the Woods
> Had power to mangle me —
> . . .

Rap does not offer this, but has its own Orphic swell, the brio of the vocal delivery set against a musical background of tremendous pressure. The new "note" of video brings to performance poetry an added dimension.

I have chosen Emily Dickinson and Rap as my paradigm because their impact on us is beyond dispute, and because though one hundred years separate them, they remain partners in the crime of canon-breaking, especially as their unlikenesses intersect in the ballad. This factor of the ballad is, in the end, an aspect of language.

The mystery of language is the workshop of most hyphenated Americans, bereft as they are of the genealogical protocols of managerial America. To them, coming as they do from marginalized communities, the vocabulary of acculturation presents hazards beyond those of mere ambition. For their poets, the result is a process of hyper-attentiveness resembling compulsion. No one studies as hard as the self-taught; overcompensation becomes gymnastic and heartfelt. Above all, they must learn to take an audience for granted where no audience may exist because they are constructing their own contexts. The discipline is not for sissies.

I have privileged the ballad only to delineate the paradigm. In simple truth all of managerial America is "unwritten tradition" to hyphenated writers. This gives them — I am thinking of figures like Pietro di Donato, Langston Hughes, William Saroyan, Richard Wright — the energy of their recency. They deliver not only literature, but news, the political act of their new-fangledness. Or, masters as they are of the art of over-compensation, they become, like John Ciardi or Alfred Kazin, dons of the national discourse while at the same time not abandoning the immigrant heritage. Who gave us a permanently inimitable translation of Dante's *Comedia*? John Ciardi. Who wrote a great classic — the account of a dreamy boy living in the Jewish Brooklyn of yesteryear—*A Walker in the City*? Alfred Kazin.

My poem "Hubie" springs from a loyal memory of World War II, when African Americans were being admitted, like test-runs, into White military units. This practice began about five years before President Truman's famous Executive Order of 1948. I try to depict the moves toward friendship of a Black Soldier, and a White Soldier.

I wanted the technique of the poem, its gears, so to speak, to propel in some iconic manner the conflict expressed in the poem's language. I have always had a fondness for friction in poetry, the way the poem fights with itself. There is as much "superstition" in this predilection of mine, which I yield to now and then, as logic, but that's how poets are. As Plato says, poets know no shame, and are not to be trusted. After several erratic starts, I decided on the rhymed couplet as my way of "driving" my point home. The couplet is spry, and amenable to emphasis. It also travels well in narrative.

By some lucky chance I recall, at almost the same moment of this decision, a canard about the rhymed couplet, the closed couplet in particular, circulated by a deconstructionist of yore. The deconstructionist stated—I am paraphrasing here, but I make my meaning plain—that the rhymed couplet exemplified in the witty, controlled verse of Alexander Pope reflected faithfully the rationality, stability, and economic control of the mercantile, imperial England of the eighteenth century. You must recognize here our old friend, "Literature is Power." I have always harbored a resentment of that theory because it besmirches my dream of language, and my respect for its mystery.

The upshot of all this is that I composed "Hubie" in what I think of as "fractured" couplets, unstable, occasionally irrational and never imperial. The couplets are closed, open, off-rhymed as well as rhymed, and the scansion of the lines is—not infrequently—impolite. The speaker of the poem, and "Hubie," are not polite characters. They are innocent, ignorant, and lost. If the poem succeeds for the reader it will do so through struggle towards some urgent truth.

I have avoided using the master-term hegemony in my comments on the canon. The actual power to "control" that hegemony signifies is ambivalently applied these days. As we are all aware there have been, for years now, efforts by federal and state governments to encourage and foster "diversity" in the schools. Philanthropic organizations, some of them quite huge, are geared toward supporting social amelioration of this kind. The temper of the times seems to indicate that a strong majority of Americans favor a national project recognizing and assisting the unrecognized and the unassisted of our marginalized communities. Unfortunately, especially in the area of cultural support—that is to say, money for the arts—these programs are racked by debates out of all proportion to the issues involved. The results of our vast national activity are still unclear.

I prefer to keep to my idea of language as the Canon behind all canons. This is something poets can understand. I conclude by appealing to young poets, assailed by thoughts of their own unlikeness, to take heart: the country of absence, where the imagination has never been, is a land where Possibility grows, like a peach in the sun.

THE COUNTRY OF ABSENCE

THE CATCH

Your college learn you be smart, talk fancy. You go with the girls, talk fancy. You tell your mother, Ma, why you got the bun on your head, old fashion. Your college learn you don't respect your mother. Some college. Now you say this girl you live together, marriage never mind, old fashion. Your mother cry, and with the beads, pray, pray, and pray. What you think, she ask me. You know what I think, boy? I think if you was pig we raise by and by we sell you for money now, not your mother cry.

TONY

Tall,
smiling-faced immigrant,
at school your handsome snickering
obsessed the rest of us.

The windows,
barred, as in prison,
looked down and gleamed at you,
which made us mad to follow
in the wake of your little scandals.
Our kind teacher
talked over our heads to you.

I remember
bouts of snobbery
when I schemed like a gambler
over my homework,
and rolled my eyes in class
at your inexorable ignorance.
Alert as a mouse
I used to loiter in the hallway
to hear
the useless reprimands
you received after class.
I scampered home,
thrilled with your shame.

Across the aisle
I ogled you like a girl.
I envied you your wild curls,

hair, that like you,
refused to stay in place.
I think I pitied you,
the holes in your shoes.

How brave,
how uselessly brave, Tony,
to dare your banishment.
What a scene at thirteen years,
you, chiding the Cyclops
to find you out.
Recalling that
plagues me now
like something choked down—
we laughed, we stamped our feet,
we hooted the principal
at her harangue,
the teacher, tears in his eyes,
who escorted you down the hall
like a jail-house priest.

Destiny, Destiny,
why were you so pretty,
so sure to die?

Before the summer was out,
and the grass dead,
you were struck down
as by a thunderbolt.

You were caught in a stolen car,
yourself the darting child you didn't see,
and iron rang in your ears.

Years later I saw you on Tenth Street,
pushing your wagon-load of fruit.
The sun seized you
like a searchlight
in our little square,
where you peddled your wares
in a brutal tremelo,
hoarse, out of breath.
Smiling-faced,
I stood before you,
blocking your way.
But you pushed around,
you stared right through me,
like a prisoner at Auschwitz,
seeing nothing but his death.

FEAST OF SAN GENNARO

And I remember figs strung on a wall,
and peppers, red and vicious, in a bowl
with thyme and fennel, on the window sill
beyond my reach, who wasn't very tall—

and sunlight spilling into the tiny room
to fall like plunder at my mother's feet
while at the table, calmly, calmly, she beat
the dough as if it were a golden drum—

and father's silly knocking at the door,
singing that Lola was his lady-love,
and chestnuts in my pockets, round and warm,
and Uncle Tony snoring by the stove—

and my fat cousins in their squeaky shoes
I can recall, and the quick, sudden pride
of my own laughter, and the wine, and how
tall yesterdays ago we never died.

THE MARIONETTES

See how they dream their wooden dreams,
pine legends in their painted eyes.
Their ardor is of crepe and chalk;
the fire is their only surprise.

Catch how they mouth their gargoyle talk;
they even love with a scratching sound.
The fire is their only surprise,
Pinocchio burning himself to the ground.

Watch how they dance their clacking dance;
their kiss is like the breaking of a box.
They would sprout leaves, like fingers of sense—
Master Gepetto, how they dance,

sauntering past with chirping knees
through the proscenium's feast of eyes.
Wanting not to be made of wood,
the fire is their only surprise.

City of iron metaphors,
your children applaud their angular pranks
as their freak noses bump in fiction.
Do they hope that mothers will offer thanks?

See how they turn their necks of bark,
wound and wired for noise and friction.

They are not children lost in the dark.
The fire is their only surprise.

Friend Cricket, like a piccolo,
you weep from the wall your prophecy:
they are so lonely racked on the shelves;
they can weep splinters if only they try.

They're not content to be themselves,
but plot a vegetable sovereignty,
with their sinister, sonorous Italian names
dreaming some varnished mythology.

The fire is their only surprise.
They court the green and yellow courtesan;
in her silver dress she is telling them lies.
The moon is their favorite citizen.

And all unsteadied by their pilgrimage
to this last boondock of a grimy town
visited by their pushcart prompt parades
I spy a hundred wooden strangers in the lemon dawn.

They are shouting I love you in an old dialect,
their chatterbox tarantellas waking the glades —
Colombina, the barking of Melampo,
the toy apples of Giuseppina's breasts,

shimmering forth from the ultimate shores of illusion,
Puncinello, staring with eyes of pearl,
singing I love the child with the blue hair,
I love the green and yellow girl.

HOW I CHANGED MY NAME, FELICE

In Italy a man's name, here a woman's,
transliterated so I went to school
for seven years, and no one told me different.
The teachers hardly cared, and in the class
Italian boys who knew me said Felice,
although outside they called me feh-LEE-tchay.

I might have lived, my noun so neutralized,
another seven years, except one day
I broke a window like nobody's girl,
and the old lady called a cop, whose sass
was wonderful when all the neighbors smiled
and said that there was no boy named Felice.
And then it was it came on me, my shame,
and I stepped up, and told him, and he grinned.

My father paid a quarter for my sin,
called me inside to look up in a book
that Felix was American for me.
A Roman name, I read. And what he said
was that no Roman broke a widow's glass,
and fanned my little neapolitan ass.

A FIG TREE IN AMERICA

They hang full jewel, clusters of ripe figs
on the soft vine, and stir like pregnant women
bothered by a breeze toward new discomforts:
in a keen ache of fullness slowly stir.

August, month of Midas, touches gold
the green branch burgled by the birds and worms
where they hang, in serious attitudes like bombs
in the heaving cockpit of my fierce remembrance:

my father, moving slowly through the ruins,
like Vergil in his baggy overalls,
to aim his spade as though it were a spear,
and kick, from a cold slum, the slags of Troy.

And here I stand, amid the brick and business,
over the ultimate exile of his grave,
to marvel at my mortal foreigner,
who struck a flag that still can fly so green.

WHO WOULD HAVE THOUGHT

(For Fred Gardaphe)

Who would have thought, I thought,
that gas light in a room
a life ago, would light this poem
my memory has wrought?

It winked across the window panes
of our pocket of a kitchen,
where I without a stitch on,
was being scrubbed for all my stains.
I paddled that dented tub
with angry rub-a-dub dub,
while father mopped the floor
and dared me to spill more.
Then mother wiped my ears,
and sang to dry my tears.
Poor father hummed along;
his voice was much too strong
for such a little ditty,
and more's the pity.

That soap-and-water swimmer
treads shadows in a dream,
though now and then a gleam
of memory casts its shimmer,
like gas light, flicker-fleeter
than skipping rhyme and meter.

FARFALLA

Once, speaking of her brother, Uncle Joe,
my mother mixed the idiom, and put
the foot before the hand in hand-and-foot,
and laughed, and went on talking even so,
about my uncle's zany one-man-show —
a singing waiter on a pleasure boat —
intoning menus with a golden throat,
and dancing three-foot platters heel and toe.

I knew the story, as I also knew
the one he told about my mother too:
how once, far from sun-spattered Italy
a snowflake waltzing down a winter sky
amazed a little girl, who joyfully
sang out then in Italian, "Butterfly!"

ANTONIO STEFANILE
Nola, Italy, 1873-1959

You were a peaceful king, with many spies.
I think of all the slow and careful strangers
walking through the streets of foreign towns
who wore on their watch-chains the gift you sent,
the little coral horn that fought bad luck.
Now you are dead, the lurching continents
seem even less safe than they were before,
so scattered are we — like the Jews, surprised
to our identity this seventh year.
In Argentina children call your name;
who is there left now, old and queer enough
to write, and give advice, and pray for us?
New York and Canada send telegrams,
but where's the Elder now of all our tribe,
the shaman, pipe and proverb, we left home?
Your strength was stubbornness, not luxury:
Anchises turned about, you carried us.
Beyond the sea's walls we remembered Troy,
and you old shade, who stalked that abandoned rubble
like a good shepherd, among sheep of stone.
In Boston an Irish priest trips on your name
to welcome to a world you had not walked
your late reality, your myth that bloomed
like mist beneath that moon of memories,
our banishment. O gentle, antique king,
of spirit large enough for large farewells,
the wind is but a roster of our names
that blow like seeds cast from your ancient earth.

CARMEN

(for Daniela Gioseffi)

Carmen, you were seven. You sought me after school,
just came alongside as I marched away,
and fell in stride. I caught your side-long glances.
Beneath your bangs and spit-curls you were pale,
your dark eyes shimmered, you were all eyes.
You talked a blue streak for a stranger,
and I hardly answered. I was shy of words.
You said you were afraid of our old streets,
men shouting at trucks backing in and out
of those huge factory gates, the eerie ring
of cobblestones, as in a spooky movie.
Day after day we walked each other home
to that last corner, where you turned away.
You said you'd cross the street, but I must watch.
I never looked for you except the day
you didn't show up, and I walked home alone.
I wondered if you'd found another friend.
Days later then I heard, while in a store,
holding the bread for mother, you were dead.
There were those women at the spice-laden counter,
saying your name in passing, as at an altar.
I listened in a daze, and looked for mother.
She said that we would stop to light a candle
on the way home at St. Mary-of-the sea.
There at the railing I picked out my candle,
and we said the ten Hail Marys, the Glory Be.
As we walked home my heart raced far ahead,
light-years ahead, I know, to this bright moment,
for now like a goddess, stronger than Diptheria,
that goddess of dead children, Carmen, you light my mind.

ANDREW

Friend, heavy survivor,
you bear the bull's lowered brow,
ready for comers.

To look at you is to understand
jungles are not nice.
My mind creates tableaux

set behind glass — don't touch —
in memory's museum,
especially one of a classroom

and teacher calling you wop.
Or that night in Linden Park
when, head lowered,

you told me your mother was dead.
We were fourteen,
completely uncomforted.

I suppose things are better today.
We are offered courses on dying.
The joggers tell us, Love yourself.

Old puff-belly baldhead,
you listen to your kids complain,
and smile.

You make a killing at the track
and zoom home in your huge car,
full of frowns.

For you a proverb might be set:
do not thank the gods too loudly,
or they will hear you and change their minds.

Brother, fellow loser,
I know why in these enlightened times
you still tend the Sacred Heart

on the wall
outside your bedroom
with fragrant candles:

it is the one trophy you understand,
as Jesus taught—
we are all nailed to the wall.

THE DAY WE DANCED THE SAINT

for Zi' Anton'

The day we danced the Saint our shoulders worked
beneath the logs, to the music of a march,
and rowdy with religion we cut loose
to try a jig with that long weight on us,
left flank together, then to the right, then left,
running a little, suddenly stopping dead:
the young girls screamed to watch our statue leap
out of its chocks, it seemed, and lean at them,
his fresh paint flashing in the sun like fire.
The band played *Stella Alpina* and we danced,
red-faced and grinning; grandmothers cackled back
clutching their black shawls, and throwing sweets
wide of the mark, crunched beneath our feet.
Where we pushed on small children ran with us,
skipping and hopping, calling a father's name,
Papa Antonio! like that, in public proof
he held his post beneath the logs that bore
our plaster Saint upon the wooden stage,
where dollars gleamed like sequins on his robe
and made a noise like feathers in the wind.
Next to me Rodolfo puffed and swore,
his face damp with religion and its work,
while up ahead fat Father Ferdinand
swung with the weight, the Pope's own pachyderm,
"*Laetantur coeli!*" roaring to our jibes.
"Don't go to heaven too soon!" Rodolfo cried,
and the logs rumbled, but our Saint stayed put.
I glimpsed my mother peering through the crush,
torn between love of Christ, love of her son,

whose skinny shoulders she feared surely would crack
beneath that holy rubble overhead,
but I straightened up, and winked, like some famous athlete,
along with big Arnaldo, Menechin,
Gaetano, Guido, Salvatore and Dino.
We came at last into the smell of wine
and cooking in the air, and the band stopped;
the crowd broke, with a splashing noise, and flags,
shot streamers, colored paper, rained on us,
and suddenly, up front, the old square shone
like a sheet of beaten gold in the noon light.

A young man, like a soldier on report,
raced up to Father Ferdinand, and shouldered
his post with a quick circus-skill that pleased
the elders gathered on the churchyard steps.
The priest walked out, and raised his hands. Shouts back
told him we owned our God that day, at least,
and with a smile he signalled to the women
waiting along the ropes, as at a race,
and they ran to us with glasses, cups and flagons,
streaming along the ranks where we stood firm,
squat, sweating Samsons, holding up our pride.
When my girl found me, as I knew she would,
her fingers thrusting mint-leaves in my mouth
and holding up the wine-flask for my kiss,
I was the purest penitent standing there,
and I dared the forty Saints to break my back.

ATLANTIS

That hunched and crowded town on the eastern coast
blinded the light of the moon with its own moonshine
and held the sea back with a cable line.
Lights technicolor, rust, and rainbow almost,
when these winked out behind me, like a ghost
I toured the night, but I was never lost.

Beyond New Jersey then, I watched hills start
and toil toward mountains, like dark lava rolled
from Alleghany's brimstone red-and-gold
of sunrise, and my eastern heart took heart
to think that the stumbling sea had no such art
to follow where the mountains make a fort.

Then sliding down Ohio's punch-bowl, toward
the Indiana corn-fields, watched them wave;
my new old prairie home made me feel brave.
And never guessed, till now, from what dark hoard
this landlocked moon that blinds me can afford
the light I lost, the sea I never heard.

Landlubber's luck, without a tide to race,
with money in my jeans, hole in my head,
I spy on strangers of squat, farmer's tread,
and wonder, for the years, how many seas
it took to sail their dream to this dry place.

That block of salt, the moon, is good and dead;
those meadows heaving in the summer rain
are not the sea I carry in my head.

I have a different kind of dream to bed,
and wrote this song, and saved my life again.

LETTER FROM A FRIEND IN EXILE

... I move among them, neither spy nor slave,
though like a spy I hoard my poverty
and like a slave I count their property
as something strange, and good, and not my own—
for what I touch here, brick, or bark, or bone,
does not touch back the way my fingers felt
the gritty answer of my crumbling hearth
the day I threw my name upon the fire
and ran my nail across the mantel's crack:
(it wandered, like a river on a map).

But that map's gone, and my lost country gone,
names of cities changed, our temples toppled.
Our children have been herded into pens,
our strong men run away to rocks and caves,
our women tossed like baggage on the shields
of the barbarian. And I am here, in exile,
ghost of a guest to all the gentle hosts.

Ingratitude? No. Thanks are in my heart:
I thank these men for the sound their footsteps make
in the safe night, for their moon's long-legged strut,
their silver Daddy puffing on his pipe
in fifty miles of corn, I thank the dawn
for happening in the sure way it does,
like a fine woman, with her apron gathered,
draping the light's clean clothes on all the lines.
I thank them when I close the door on them,
and hear their voices laughing down the hall,
then fading, as though voices became birds,
and fussed upon the branches, and grew still.

Like eager mutes, the shadows talk to me,
and in the darkness all my shades agree.

But what man needs a friend who will not grieve
when it is time for him to grieve, a friend
who puts his war too soon away from him?
If home is where the heart is, as you say,
then I still burn for my own broken hearth.
You must forgive this, as the sun forgives
the balked raid of the night on your bright fields.

IN THAT FAR COUNTRY

> The clouds are streaming in the sky, like birds.
> The leaves are falling to the ground, like rain.
> My house, unhawsered in the autumn wind,
> Creaks like the ship that took me far from home.
> — *Selma Stefanile*

In that far country formed of coves and bays,
and clouds that float like swans across the sky,
where nothing happens history can praise
or blame, because there is no history,
I read the sun's handwriting on a wall
of ivied hieroglyphs, I spy a town
where the seasons gracefully return and fall
as in a sanctuary all my own.
The language that they speak is greek to me
in that still land. Only the children run;
the women weave their nets besides the sea;
the old men suck their pipes beneath the sun;
and people gather in the village square
to ask about me, why I am not there.

ULISSE, *by Umberto Saba*

Nella mia giovanezza ho navigato
lungo le coste dalmate. Isolotti
a fior d'onda emergevano, ove raro
un ucello sostava intento a prede,
coperti d'alghe, scivolosi, al sole
belli come smeraldi. Quando l'alta
marea e la notte annullava, vele
sottovento sbandavano più al largo
per fuggirne l'insidia. Oggi il mio regno
è quella terra di nessuno. Il porto
accende ad altri i suoi lumi, me al largo
sospinge ancora il non domato spirito,
e della vita il doloroso amore.

UMBERTO SABA: ULYSSES

When I was young I sailed the Dalmatian coast.
Great islands bloomed on the wave; above them flew
once in a while a bird in search of prey.
Covered with kelp, and slippery, under the sun
they shone as beautiful as emeralds.
When night came, and in the high tide they vanished,
with our sails underwind we ducked for the deep
to flee that perilous snare. Today, like that,
my kingdom is No Man's Land. My harbor
burns lanterns for foreigners, and I turn back to sea,
pressed ever on by my unbeaten spirit,
and by my broken-hearted love of life.

translated by Felix Stefanile

CECCO ANGIOLIERI (1260?-1313)

Mie madre si m'insegna medicina
la qual non m'è crudelmente, sana:
che' mmi dice ch'i' usi a la campana
da otto pesche o diece la mattina,

che mmi faran campar de la contina
e di febbre quartan' e di terzana;
molto mi loda l'anguille di chiana,
che 'l cap' e me' ch' otriaca fina.

Carne di bu' e cascio e cipolle
molte me loda, quand'i' sento doglia,
e ch'i' ne faccia ben buona satolla;

e se di questo non avessi voglia,
e stessi quasimente su la colla,
molto mi loda porri con le foglia.

CECCO COMPLAINS ABOUT HIS MOTHER'S CURE-ALL

(For Paolo Giordano)

My mother brings me up on medicine
that sad to tell does not agree with me,
though with the morning bells I dutifully
choke down her breakfast of eight pears or ten,

to keep the plague away, and hex, and pain,
the fever of the four days or the three.
Alas, with me, I find that eels agree:
one eel is worth all cures that famish men.

And I find beef, and cheese, and onions too,
they really go down well when I feel bad;
with such a bellyful I can make do.

But when recuperation can't be had,
and my prognosis is, at best, quite sad,
I mix them up with greens, and make a stew.

translated by Felix Stefanile

ON A REMARK BY THE POET, DANA GIOIA, ON TRANSLATING

> Translation is inevitable, in the first place,
> because of the curse of Babel...
> — *Robert M. Adams*

It is sheer coveting, that much is clear,
of someone else's folly and surprise,
and soothes your secret fever as you peer
into another person's heart, to see
with calm, untroubled eyes,
how things may be and how things may not be.
The act of a voyeur,
you spy a fellow out, and take his lies
for granted, your own motives less than pure.
Then you fix his measure, take a look
in a strange dictionary, and try your luck.

Out of the poem you gingerly extract
the live-coal from the clinker in the grate;
then envy glosses into cunning tact,
the shimmering in your hands. By fits and starts
you ponder, study, weigh, you extricate
from gritty clots the gleaming private parts.
Soon it's like keeping score;
your pencil flails away, moods don't distract,
and the grisly business leaves no trace of gore.
When you are finished, watch him strut and rage;
it isn't you that's crying in the cage.

This will not do for Homer, you've been told,
or Dante. Shakespeare has the best of it

for changing englished Plutarch into gold.
That wasn't alchemy, but outright theft.
No doubt our mother wit
does well enough—though we are all bereft
since Babel's shame—
to strike a phrase cast from our own stronghold,
but you're translating now, so stake your claim—
we're babbling foreigners all, and none the worse
for Bibles put to native prose and verse.

THE DANCE AT ST. GABRIEL'S

for Louis Otto

We were the smart kids of the neighborhood
where, after high school, no one went to school,
you NYU and I CCNY.
We eyed each other at St. Gabriel's
on Friday nights, and eyed each other's girls.
You were the cute, proverbial good catch
— just think of it, nineteen — and so was I,
but all we had was moonlight on our minds.
This made us cagey; we would meet outside
to figure how to dump our dates, go cruising.
In those hag-ridden and race-conscious times
we wanted to be known as anti-fascists,
and thus get over our Italian names.
When the war came, you volunteered, while I
backed in by not applying for deferment,
for which my loving family named me Fool.
Once, furloughs overlapping, we met up,
the Flight Lieutenant and the PFC;
we joked about the pair we made, and sauntered.
That Father Murray took one look at us,
and said our Air Force wings were the only wings
we'd ever earn. We lofted up our beers.
Ah, Louis, what good times we two have missed.
Your first time up and out the Germans had you,
and for your golden wings they blew you down.

SOLDIERS AND THEIR GIRLS

(First Three-Day Pass)

Those years before Fast Food a pizza meant
a neighborhood, an accent maybe, or
the way the customers looked. You had your limits.
One train-stop more it might be Fish and Chips,

or Blintzes. What a way to spend a date,
skipping from joint to joint, and getting drunk
on laughter and strange sipping, stupid jokes
about the squid, rose-water, or flat-bread.

Whatever, down it went. You smiled and smiled
because the girl was pretty and proud
and scared. She wanted you to know
Armenians were just like you, or Jews,

and we were all Americans anyway.
You checked your watch, said "Hitler!" She teared up,
pert Rosie Ohanessian, whose large eyes
were darker than that last night on your mind.

She walked you to the depot. You held hands,
but never made a move, the station crammed,
young couples slouching, grinning, waiting for
the speaker to announce the bus from camp.

BALLAD OF THE WAR BRIDE

Willie, on leave, got married, and came home
to show his discharge, and show off his bride,
a gangling, giggling girl from Birmingham
without a cent. His mother almost died.

His father came right out and talked expense,
and told them that this wasn't Alabam.
The kids agreed. As if doing penance
they both found jobs, and soon the money came.

His mother grumbled on, as did his father;
they said they couldn't understand her speech.
A girl with yellow hair was too much bother,
and they were sure that she was using bleach.

One day they told him, fever in their eyes,
"Kick in more money, and we'll save for you."
Then it was that Willie, past surprise,
knew what he and his sweetheart had to do.

One morning, trim deportment a pure sham,
they left for work as far as one could tell,
but with train tickets back to Birmingham.
He called his folks en route, and told them go to hell.

HONORABLE ARMY DISCHARGE

My heart was full of money, and my head
was full of dreams, the day that I got home
for good. My mother cried and cried, my sisters
cried; my brother, turned fourteen, just stared
and laughed, and stuck his finger to his head
and rolled his eyes. It was as if to say
that things were back to normal now, and crazy.

When Pop came home from work, harroomph, harroomph,
he asked me if I'd been to see my room,
the new paint job. He tripped upon a word,
said something about a new bloom sweeping clean.

That broke things up, we laughed, we all sat down
to eat and talk. I choked the pasta down
as best I could; it was so rich and sweet,
the taste of a largesse I had forgotten.
I never guessed at yearning, those lost years,
until late in the night. The new paint job
seared through my nostrils, and brought out the tears,
my room so small, so safe, so quiet I heard
the drumming in my ears, my heart's own cannon
time and again go whoosh and whoosh and thud.

BACK HOME IN INDIANA

I get home,
like Charlie Chaplin,
all my dirigibles floating.

Gimpy from work
I sit, and drink, and think
there is much sailing to be done in Indiana —
at least one good ocean to dig,
some seventy thousand sea-gulls to be imported
and the right kind of foreigner, the wrong kind,
with black hair, gold teeth and a lucky parrot.

Across the Wabash one day
I'd heard Mexican field-hands, their delicate noise:
real Indians in Tippecanoe County,
right next to the Methodist Church.

Montauk! Montauk!
I cried, in my mind's leap,
thinking of that last page
in *The Great Gatsby* —
the homeless shore,
naked, unnamed,
the dunes of Long Island swirled like carpets
ready for the tread of Europe.

And here, in the central plain, the final result:
history, a cleared table;
corn, heaped up like bullion, like the cross-over vote.
Safe from the pull of the tide and the smell of the moon
there is no rocking the boat in Indiana.

TO BE FRANK ABOUT IT

(For Anthony J. Tamburri)

Lord of the loser, and the truant's god,
a hellbent high school dropout fast for ruin,
he didn't end up shining shoes. Instead,
Fame licked his boots, and women licked their lips.
Saints walk through walls. Sinatra was no saint,
and yet he soared through ceilings like a wisp,
the electronic angel of an age,
on wings of song, despite the smoker's cough.
The cleaned out gambler, the receptionist
who falls in love each time a dream walks in
and puts his briefcase down, and smiles at her,
the cousins from Hoboken pray to him.
Now he has vanished, old-time columnists
punch their computers blind to find the words
to put him down, the magic and the madness
that summoned armies. Envy stares, aghast,
to think this swaggering, crass evangelist
who came from cobbled streets and cold room flats
should sing of heaven where no heaven was,
in Babylon and Hollywood and home,
the place where such thoughts last. There some young girl,
some old coot who is kicking off his shoes
to clear his head, is listening to the songs.
It is the jaunty fox who now must weep,
and weep the longest. If Audacity
goes down, what shall we tell the little ones
of courage and persistence, and the hunt
that keeps them hungry and that keeps them fed?

TAKING SIDES WITH JOHN CIARDI

— some words on minus-American poetry

When Robert Lowell hyphenated you —
Italian, hyphen sign, American —
to praise your poetry, your answer ran
in rough-house expletives. Your passion flew,
and subsequently in an interview
you squelched his harmless seeming little hyphen
as not the way to write out citizen.
How culture-vultures smiled at the to-do.

If this is poetry, as may be true,
it's also punctuation, not too thin
a point or line for morals that you drew.
We all know grammar can stick like a pin,
and those who think my point is overdrawn,
they are no friends of yours, nor of mine, John.

A POEM FOR SELMA

Water dripping: the insatiable voice
of the radio, sarcastic bee
buzzing through the cheap sunlight of our rooms;
the hall, dark as a warehouse, and our clothes
slumped over chairs, in silent, dreadful poses,
crumpled flags
slipped in a sudden ambush; piles of books
scattered, as slate torn in the morning wind
of our hurry—all, all our choice and chattel,
and we make for it, each night, from the long train
dumping us, like troops, to a dim outpost
in the domestic jungle of our lives.

That grouch, my shadow, waylays every move
she makes, for booby-traps galore
flickering under touch: the pillows staled;
papers, like clues, under the bed; cracked combs
her fingers cannot heal,
and the smell of a crazy kitchen
where she burns to know the woman that she is.

Canned goods, in rhymes of color, stacked on shelves,
remember landscapes dreamed unleft
in the lucky midnight when our sleep was sound.
The clock, like rivers, flowed. The alley dripped
Babylon, and the rain fell—
moss on the wall, and mushrooms in the brick.

There is conspiracy in all these smells:
pine in the soap and talcum in the bleach,

whore's air of roses in the insecticide,
all the expensive junk of cleanliness.

The ugliness of this poem is my love:
I think how even the germs are frightened by it.

Outside, a code of spectrums on the street
holy my prison with the prism's soul.
I remember that morning waking, dizzily floating,
thrashing through swirling sheets toward reality's mud,
a paper-swimmer, tearing on the rocks of morning.

I tugged at the fur
of my long beast dream,
but the dog's nose was cold.

I staggered toward linoleum reefs
where my sun was, shining
in rich, aluminum stripes
on the radiator.

And then you woke, in that iron-colored air,
saying, It's time, not, as I ask,
Is it time?
In the distance, over the rusty shacks of the morning,
that crooked map shaped in reliefs of gravel,
we heard a rooster crying impossibly,
and he was saying Peacock, Peacock, Peacock.

EMILY

> Should mortal lips divine
> The undeveloped freight
> Of a delivered syllable
> 'T would crumble with the weight.
> — *Emily Dickinson*

We know that Emily would place a finger
upon a letter in a word, and linger,
lost in imagination's curlicues,
because a friend had sent her pretty news.

Words, the syllables, the sounds, the grace
of penmanship, or how lines danced with space
across a page, it was to catch their gist
she peered and peered, merry cabalist.

She once confessed she kept herself away
from opening an envelope all day
to read the vision her denial spun.
Anticipation warmed her like the sun.

Spry angel, safe in heaven, when upstairs,
but kitchen heretic, she put on airs
and thought of poems while baking father's cake.
The light through the window slanted for her sake.

Merry and naught, and gay and numb, she wrote
about herself. She had the antidote:
she tracked the moth beneath the metaphor;
then East and West, like hinges, swung a door.

Coy hymnodist, who rarely went to church,
her meter never left her in the lurch.
As for the tunes, Revival cast its moods,
and her piano echoed through the woods.

She cobbled up her verse on scraps of paper;
how they ignited from her flickering taper —
a gleaming galaxy of joy and doubt,
some worlds put in, and some worlds put to rout.

She stitched the scraps of paper into sheaves,
and pressed them down, like folded handkerchiefs,
into a chest her father never saw.
Ah, what a dowry for the Bride of Awe!

Some she mailed out, as pert as valentines,
to friends and relatives. Like ore in mines
they hid in attics, albums, cellar murk,
until uncovered by the digger's work.

I praise these archeologists of craft
who piece shards together she had left,
the daft and deft designs, the blinding jewel
tucked in the folds of an old, forgotten shawl.

Old Untermeyer, in his anthology,
said neighbors thought her but an oddity.
She had the great misfortune, and the will,
to be — unlike her neighbors — original.

Now scholars, out to get her with their praises,
bedeck her with their own outlandish phrases.
One well meant term for her is "heroinism,"
but Emily was her own neologism.

She stays, the mistress of her mystery,
despite our good intentions: Emily,
who said, "My business is Circumference,"
still wore her skin around her like a fence.

Ah, Emily, forgive our late respect:
Americans are never circumspect.
We shower you with our own mad surprise;
you disappeared before our very eyes.

Forgive me too, who make a clumsy case.
I've borrowed from you, and purloined your grace.
Forgive me, if you can, sad Muse, my small gray dove,
for my presumption, but not for my love.

HUBIE

> *Army experiments with*
> *mixed units: Negroes being*
> *admitted into white*
> *companies.*
> — News Item 1943

You, Hubie, were the one and only black
in our whole crazy outfit. You had a knack
for fending off our clumsy comradeship.
You were a ferret at a Freudian slip
or condescension: (let's ask Hubie, too!)
You always answered, "Cut it out, will you?"
Except one time: the night we made to go
to the Anselmo Club, and wouldn't you know,
we challenged you, we forced you, kidnapped you
to come along. You came. We wrecked the place.
The frightened 4F doorman mentioned race,
held his hand up to his pasty face,
and said you had no card, no "membership."
He tried to close the door; Paul knocked his grip,
and hollered, "He's our guest!" Then the poor guy said No,
and Paul, half drunk already, just let go.
That was a fight we all enjoyed but you;
the cops came, and your black skin saved our hides,
because the owner blamelessly denied
that there was trouble, and we made no news.
No news was good for him, and good for us,
but the drink you drank that night was bitter, bitter juice.

Then there was Captain Jones from Millidgeville
(Gee-AY!) who hated you so hard it killed

to hear him give you his Boy-this, Boy-that.
He hated all of us, but that was pure so what
to the dockside bruisers, city toughs,
and all the ill-assorted country roughs
that made up our sad clan of prison-chasers:
we knew that you were the true King of Losers.
Maybe that's why we liked you, let that stay,
from ignorance to shame to light of day.
Jones ran us like a chain-gang, that's for sure,
but your bland moon-face shone, "Endure, endure."

Once I glimpsed you with the Enemies.
It was their singing time. They were a breeze
to guard, no trouble. It was a heavy night
of stars and blooms, of shadows that turned bright.
A kid cupped his right hand up to his face
the way they did to magnify the voice,
and winked at you. Hubie, you winked back.
It was a sign between you for a song,
and then he gave their yodel, loud and long,
fronni e limoni, which maybe signified
some legend lost when ancient glory died,
but left its echo. No one would begin
before the signal, *lemon leaves*, had run
in gross annunciation. The same phrase
would introduce each stanza. In a daze
I heard the eerie music, though this time
the voice I heard was yours, in Neapolitan rhyme,
and my translation of it is a crime:

Oh leaves of the lemon trees! It's in the shape of crosses
they are constructed, all the gates of prison,
the better to destroy the sons of mothers.
Ah, Hubie, what a maundering in my heart

to hear you go falsetto, sob and start,
and grace-note the muezzin-vaunt of words,
gliding the vowels over, like slow birds,
the drawn out line. I thought my head would burst.
For their lament those lads made you sing first;
you knew the chant; it could have been the blues,
three lines of heartbreak, blood down to your shoes.
Then came the answers, in the same old notes,
one fellow, then another, golden throats —
tears for a mother, or a girl back home,
some nasty verse on the Pope in Rome,
and when your turn came round again you sang
about the way the bells of Nola rang.
Mad Captain Jones's "damn eye-talian crew"
had caught your grave compassion, trusted you,
and taught you more Italian for a song
than the rest of us had learned the whole year long.
Those distant bells, they did you no more good,
than did the chimes of elegant Englewood,
New Jersey, where you came from, preacher's son,
out of a tiny Baptist congregation
made up of cooks and gardeners, garbage men,
and other service people all hemmed in.
The war came, you were ready, just like me,
which meant no job, no future, and no money.

What now comes back to me, old Hubie, is
how you and I could sit and shoot the breeze
those Sunday afternoons, when things went dead
in repple-depple camp. The peace went to my head.
We chuckled about week-end roll-calls, played
the same each muster: mostly no one up
except us cowards who were thin on hope,
afraid to miss the check and rate KP,

although in truth half our company
slept through. The guys took turns as stand-ins, one
for every two or three in mock attention,
answering for O'Toole or Policetti
or Garbatino. Sergeant Parmelee
stared straight down at his pad, and called the lot,
then swung around to go back to his cot.
"Why don't you slack off, Hubie?" I asked once.
You snorted, as though you took me for a dunce,
patted my knee with that ham hand of yours,
and said, "Because for me it would just be my arse.
With my complexion can't you see the fun?"
The simple truth fell on me like a ton.

Poor twins, we were discharged on the same day,
a lot to do, pick up our pay,
strip down our cots — "They might just change their minds,"
our sergeant snarled, "so move your fat behinds" —
sweep out the years, go listen to the lecture
on Re-enlistment and Reserve, some double feature;
then scoot to chow, and back to Camp Supply.

The Quartermaster goof-off, Sleepy Eye,
just brushed our gear aside, and made us sign.
On our way out we passed a clothing bin;
talk about brave! I knew we were civilians
when I snitched a cap, an Eisenhower jacket,
and so did you, you bum, and you said, "Fuck it."
The whole platoon was gone when we got back,
the silence of the barracks pure whip-crack
of memories in my head, I stared at you.
You said, "There's still one thing for us to do,"
and handed me a sheet, hodge-podge
of name, address, and Bible verse for pledge

all loyalty, no betrayal. To make things worse
I read aloud that thundering, crying verse,
because you told me once I was a poet.
What boobs we were; how kind we didn't know it.
I handed you a map of streets, instructions,
accompanied by four-letter imprecations
of what would happen if you didn't write me,
or come and visit. Then you'd have to fight me.
The map showed names of streets and bus route numbers.
All at once we stopped. We were struck dumb.
You blinked your eyes, and made a choking noise.
That was enough for me; I lost my voice.

We neither of us wrote. What came
between? It was not a forgetting. It was time
that took its aim, and brought us down like fools.
We had survived — according to the rules —
the deaths, the separations, all the cant
of war, of honor, and the special rant
of patriotism. We had saved our skins
through years of soldiering, the tightrope dance
of danger, boredom, whatever we fought for;
ourselves, we knew, were the true spoils of war.
We moved from that into the orgy of
the personal release of pure self-love.

The time is gone for what we should have said
or done, old Hubie. All the dead are dead.
Time was once ripe. Now time's a rotten thought.
Yet blow me down, and scratch me for an ought,
we buddied to the end, just to endure.
(There is a thought here that is less than pure.)

A black man and a white man, that's for sure,

this other war, and the cagey cowardice
of habit, turning honest blood to ice.
I think that we were brothers once, "The Twins,"
the fellows called us, masking their wide grins.
What's left is poetry, the penance for my sins.

THE AMERICANIZATION OF THE IMMIGRANT

Your words, Genoveffa,
through the open window,
telling me once again
what to buy at the store—
don't forget, don't forget—
aroma of fresh bread
almost a halo.

That was a long time ago.
I never forgot.
Like Dante
I have pondered and pondered
the speech I was born to,
lost now, mother gone,
the whole neighborhood bull-dozed,
and no one to say it on the TV,
that words are dreams.

ABOUT THE AUTHOR

Felix Stefanile was born in 1920 in Long Island City, New York. He was educated in the public schools and at CCNY. A World War II veteran, he found employment after the war in a series of clerical jobs until 1950, when he began his eleven-year stint in the New York State Department of Labor. There he eventually became a middle functionary in worker's claims and entitlements. In 1954 he and his wife Selma started the poetry magazine *Sparrow*, which is now one of the oldest poetry journals in the United States. His essay, "The Imagination of the Amateur," which expresses his ideas on independent literary publishing in American history was published in 1966. The essay gained him a National Endowment for the Arts Prize in 1967, and has been anthologized.

In 1961, Felix Stefanile was invited by Purdue University to serve as Visiting Poet and Lecturer for one year. At the end of his tenure, the university asked him to stay on as a member of the English faculty. He taught freshman composition, survey courses, and a Poetry Writing class that drew campus-wide attention. In 1969 he was appointed to a Full Professorship, and in 1973 was awarded the Standard Oil of Indiana Prize for Best Teacher. His poetry awards include the Emily Clark Balch Prize of the *Virginia Quarterly Review* in 1972. In 1997 he was the first recipient of the recently established John Ciardi Award for life-long achievement in Italian American poetry.

Afterword

by

Dana Gioia

Afterword

Felix Stefanile was a distinguished poet, translator, editor, and critic. He published seven books of verse as well as three significant volumes of verse translation. For forty-six years, Stefanile and his wife Selma also edited *Sparrow*, one of the liveliest poetry magazines of the era. During this long editorial tenure, he became a spokesman for the "little magazine" movement. In 1961 Stefanile, who had been working as a civil servant at the New York State Department of Labor, began teaching at Purdue University where he eventually became a full professor. He won a Balch Prize, a Pushcart Prize, and an NEA literary award. In 1998 he became the first recipient of the John Ciardi Award for lifetime achievement in Italian American poetry. Despite his many accomplishments, however, Stefanile never became widely known as a writer. He was not quite obscure, but he remained an outsider to the poetry establishment.

Stefanile's outsider status was not so much accidental as deliberate. Although he would surely have enjoyed greater visibility in literary circles, he was too independent, frank, and contrarian for much success in literary politics. Personable and notably generous to other writers, Stefanile nonetheless cultivated the identity of the amiable but uncompromising outsider. The role suited him because it reflected who he really was—a writer of high standards who didn't bend them for his own or anyone else's sake.

Stefanile was an editor who tried to make a difference. *Sparrow* began in 1954, when the mainstream of American poetry was formalist. He made the journal a home for free verse in the tradition of William Carlos Williams. The Stefaniles published Cid Corman, Robert Creeley, John Haines, George Hitchcock, and even Charles Bukowski. In 1992, however, Stefanile relaunched the journal as a magazine of the sonnet. Since free verse was now the fashionable style, he characteristically took up arms for the embattled minority.

As a poet, Stefanile presents a series of interesting paradoxes. He was both a nationalist and a cosmopolitan. Although he consciously worked in "the American grain," his poetry was nourished by deep roots in European literature. He championed free verse but also wrote in form. From his earliest work till his final publications, he was unwilling to give up one mode for the other. In *The Dance at St. Gabriel's* (1995), for instance, one finds a prose poem, a sonnet, free verse, blank verse, and rhymed quatrains side by side. A lifelong student of Italian Renaissance literature, Stefanile was an unapologetic traditionalist, but he was also an advocate of the avant-garde. He translated and published the first anthology of Italian Futurist poetry in English, *The Blue Moustache* (1981). Finally, Stefanile was a determined individualist who nonetheless always viewed himself as part of a community—ethnic, social, political, and cultural.

In these contradictory qualities, Stefanile was quintessentially an Italian-American artist, the product of a culture that combines tribal loyalty with anarchistic independence, reverence for the past with a passion for innovation. Born in 1920, he was part of a pioneering generation of writers born in this country to immigrant parents, raised speaking a foreign language, spiritually shaped by the Roman Catholic Church (even if they eventually left it), weathered by the Great Depression and World War II, educated far beyond the level of their parents, and then set loose upon the world. Both streetwise and book-smart, these young men and women entered a literary culture that simultaneously seemed both foreign and familiar. They chose to assimilate but only up to a point. As children of stoical and clannish Southern Italy, they never entirely trusted the institutions of authority.

Stefanile articulated the feisty resentment of Italian American writers toward the literary establishment in his sonnet, "Taking Sides with John Ciardi." He recounts a condescending remark Robert Lowell, the most celebrated poet of his generation and scion of a famous WASP family, made about Ciardi's work. Stefanile then "takes sides," endorsing Ciardi's anger at being marginalized as a "minus-American" poet. Like Ciardi, he refuses to accept second-class status in American letters or the snobbism of the literary establishment:

> We all know grammar can stick like a pin,
> and those who think my point is overdrawn,
> they are no friends of yours, or friends of mine, John.

The central theme of Stefanile's poetry is the complexity, surprise, and mutability of the Italian American experience. "Even though I insist on calling myself an American writer of Italian descent," Stefanile claimed in a 1993 *VIA* interview, "I believe that one of the sturdiest elements in my work is the Italian/American theme." Like so many other Italian-

American writers, he explored himself by pondering the social and cultural forces that had shaped him, his family, and his era.

What makes Stefanile's poetry outstanding among his many first-generation contemporaries was his refusal to simplify or caricature his difficult Americanization. William Wordsworth gave his autobiographical epic, *The Prelude*, the subtitle, "The Growth of a Poet's Mind," which implied both the personal and general significance of his narrative. Stefanile suggested a similar double perspective—quite Catholic in its insistence of the continuity between the visible and invisible realms of existence--when he told *Contemporary Authors*, "Art shapes life into form, in understandable and useable relation to spirit." His poems display the drive for comprehension, articulation, and transformation of life in relation to the spirit. Stefanile strived for *claritas* (to borrow a term from another Italian writer, Thomas Aquinas)--not "clarity" in the sense of the English cognate but instead "a shining forth" of an object's true essence. What Stefanile took from both his Renaissance masters and visionary Futurists was the notion that epiphanic moments, however small, were an essential element of lyric poetry. Whether in free or formal verse, a poem must "shine forth" in a form that offers an "understandable and useful" vision of existence.

Songs of the Sparrow contains all of Felix Stefanile's poetry in the original formats in which it appeared—reproducing all seven collections from a *River Full of Craft* (1956) to *The Country of Absence* (2000). This editorial decision creates some repetition due to Stefanile's habit of reprinting older poems in new contexts, but this minor problem is more than offset by the virtue of having all of Stefanile's poetry gathered together for the first time. All published by small presses, these fugitive volumes are now extremely difficult and expensive to obtain, if one can find them at all. Bordighera Press is to be congratulated for this important act of restoration.

What emerges in *Songs of the Sparrow* is a poet of superb craft and humane imagination. Reading through half a century of work, the reader finds no period of apprenticeship, nor any sense of later decline. Stefanile's first book contains what may be his finest poem, "The Marionettes," and his subsequent books are full of gems, such as "A Fig Tree in America," "Elegy, 1942," and "The Day We Danced the Saint." Stefanile stands as one of the finest Italian American writers of his generation. Like Ciardi, he brought new voices and new subjects into American literature. His vibrant and immediate poems demonstrate that to be rooted in real places doesn't make a poet parochial. Seen with a poet's eye, Queens and Brooklyn are no less universal than Oxford or Cambridge. Stefanile brought the experience of millions of American immigrants — and not just Italians — into poetry for the first time. Isn't it finally time he gets a hearing?

— Dana Gioia

INDEX OF POEMS AND ESSAYS

Advice to a Courtly Lover, 250
After cummings, 244
The Afternoon as an Aria, 11, 142
Agent's Report, 81
The Allegory of the Hyphen. An Essay, 351
American Aubade, 236
American D.P., 137
The Americanization of the Immigrant, 274, 411
American Legend, 190
Andrew, 326, 378
Anthem, 209
Antonio Stefanile, 112, 376
As I Went Out One Morning, 9, 106
Atlantis, 98, 382
At the Widow Kate's Retirement Banquet, 295
Aubade for Paquette, 139
Autumn: Indiana, 318

Back Home in Indiana, 144, 397
Ballad of the War Bride, 281, 395
Ballade of the Sad Celebrities, 283
Bal Tabarin, 21
Belting a Song, 130
Binary Rhymes, 322
The Bocce Court on Lewis Avenue, 300, 304
The Boy and the Shrike, 330
Brown, All of the Autumn, 32, 117

The Butcher Boy, 61, 133

Calm Day, 35
Carmen, 377
A Cartoon for Aristotle, 193
The Catch, 273, 365
Cecco Angiolieri, 389
Cecco Complains About His Mother's Cure-all, 390
Cheering Amy Lowell On, 289
City of Iron Metaphors, 7
Color and Line, 40
Conversation in a Storm, 143
The Country of Absence, 343
A Critique of Dante, 251

The Dance at St. Gabriel's, 267, 277, 393
Dawn, 237
The Day We Danced the Saint, 171, 380
Days Which Enchant Us, 47
December, 1941, 275
The Doge's Palace, 23
A Domestic Notion, for Selma, 29, 127
Driving East, Thinking of Frank O'Hara, 291

East River Nocturne, 20, 159, 178
Edie, 279
Egotist, 64
Elegy, 1942, 331
Elegy for My Father, 37, 153

Elegy for Yuri Gagarin and
    Others, 146
Emily, 402
Exiles, 173
Eye, 27
The Eye, 30

Fall of Adam, 45
Farfalla, 375
Feast of San Gennaro, 39, 103,
    369
A Fig Tree in America, 67, 73,
    100, 373
Fioretti, 16
For My Dark Lady, 116, 229
For My Own Birthday, 71
The Fortune Hunter, 124
From a Journal, 220
From an Apartment House
    Window, 321
Fuisse / Andrea Zanzotto, 212
Fuisse / Translation, 214

Geographies, 313
Getting Rid of My Old Virgil
    School-Text, 211
The Girl in the Garden, 132, 231
Gossip, 246
Grandfather's Story, 270
Grasshopper, 105

Hanging Out, 272
Hometown, 65, 94, 184, 238
Honorable Army Discharge,
    339, 396
How I Changed My Name,
    Felice, 63, 87, 372
Hubie, 333, 405

The Hunters, 319
Hurricane, 123

I Fond Me a Lover, 44
An Incident in Flushing Bay,
    119
The Insect World, 324
Insomniac, 56
In That Far Country, 195, 225,
    252, 386
In the Sea's Alchemies, 33
Invocation to the Muse, 89
Irises, 323
It Rains in the Neighborhoods
    of Epiphany, 234

Landmarks, 240
A Late Elegy for a Baseball
    Player, 15, 86
The Leave-Taking, 53
Letter From a Friend in Exile,
    134, 384
The Light-Bringer, 271
Lines From a Poet in Residence,
    247
A Litany, 154
The Loser's Club, 167
A Lullaby for a Dark Night, 138
L'Ultima Rinunzia, 282

Malespina, 49, 125
The Man With the Latvian
    Look, 108
The Marionettes, 12, 128, 297,
    370
Marty to Marian, 243
The Metaphysics of Winter, 328
Midwest Fantasy, 316

The Motel at the End of the Ramp, 325
Mrs. Clotho, Mrs. Lachesis, 121
Muse: Love and War, 206
Muse: To Write it Down, 186
My Long Lost Brother, 66, 104

An Old Bootblack in the Cafeteria, 19, 88
The Old Clothes Tree, 315
The Old House, 241
Old Mr. Skirmish, 70, 93
An Old Reunion, 43
On a Remark by the Poet, Dana Gioia, on Translating, 293, 391
On Family Quarrels, 242
On My Day Off a Grouchy Poem, 82
On the Mightiness of Love (Sonnet I), 249
On Painting a Bike, 320
On Theory and Practice, 269
On the Vanity of Human Wishes, 196
On the Vanity of Wisdom, 239

Paradise, 235
The Patience That Befell, 59
Poem in the Manner of Wallace Stevens, 194
A Poem for Selma, 68, 90, 400
Postcard from N.Y., 218
Proem, 169

The Quiet Man, 216

The Reporters, 113

Rewriting the Cagney and Lacey Show, 285
Riding the Storm, 205
River Full of Craft, 1

Scene for a Light Opera, 46
Scenes for a Light Opera, 41
Sea Gulls, 118
Services, 85
Slum, 176
Snow Bound, 151
Soldiers and Their Girls, 278, 394
Some Mentors, 288
Some Songs for Billie Holiday, 101
Song, 25
A Song for Rory, 232
Sonnet 3, 245
Spiaggia, 54
Spoiled by All My Tyrants, 31, 296
Spring: The Mourning Dove, 316
Street Scene: The Drunk, 136
The Suburb, 210
Summer: August, 317
Sunday Morning, 110

Taking Sides with John Ciardi, 290, 399
That Underground Sun, 57, 150
This Suicide, 17
To Answer Robert Frost, 288
To Be Frank About It, 398
Tony, 366
To Wish, 34

Ulisse, by Umberto Saba, 387
Ulysses, 329
Ulysses Arrives, 177
Ulysses, by Umberto Saba, 388
Umberto Saba, 329

The Veteran, 340
Village on My Back, 38

The Weather Didn't Do Us Any
  Good, 188
"When Longing Overcomes
  You, Sing of Great Love" —
  Rilke, 219
Who Would Have Thought,
  374
Winter: Red's Barbershop, 316
Winter Year, 51
A Word to Maecenas, in His
  Park, 230

Years, 156
You, Cowper, in Your Garden,
  62, 92
You, Poet, in Your Garden, 233

VIA FOLIOS
A refereed book series dedicated to the culture of Italians and Italian Americans.

FRANK POLIZZI. *A New Life with Bianca.* Vol 102 Poetry. $12
GIL FAGIANI. *Stone Walls.* Vol 101 Poetry. $14
LOUISE DESALVO. *Casting Off.* Vol 100 Fiction. $22
MARY JO BONA. *I stop waiting for You.* Vol 99 Poetry. $12
RACHEL GUIDO DEVRIES. *Stati zitt, Josie.* Vol 98 Children's Literature. $8
GRACE CAVALIERI. *The Mandate of Heaven.* Vol 97 Poetry. $14
MARISA FRASCA. *Via incanto.* Vol 96 Poetry. $12
DOUGLAS GLADSTONE. *Carving a Niche for Himself.* Vol 95 History. $12
MARIA TERRONE. *Eye to Eye.* Vol 94 Poetry. $14
CONSTANCE SANCETTA. *Here in Cerchio* Vol 93 Local History. $15
MARIA MAZZIOTTI GILLAN. *Ancestors' Song* Vol 92 Poetry. $14
DARRELL FUSARO. *What if Godzilla Just Wanted a Hug?* Vol ? Essays. $TBA
MICHAEL PARENTI. *Waiting for Yesterday: Pages from a Street Kid's Life.* Vol 90 Memoir. $15
ANNIE LANZILOTTO, *Schistsong,* Vol. 89. Poetry, $15
EMANUEL DI PASQUALE, *Love Lines,* Vol. 88. Poetry, $10
CAROSONE & LOGIUDICE. *Our Naked Lives.* Vol 87 Essays. $15
JAMES PERICONI. *Strangers in a Strange Land: A Survey of Italian-Language American Books.* Vol. 86. Book History. $24
DANIELA GIOSEFFI, *Escaping La Vita Della Cucina,* Vol. 85. Essays & Creative Writing. $22
MARIA FAMÀ, *Mystics in the Family,* Vol. 84. Poetry, $10
ROSSANA DEL ZIO, *From Bread and Tomatoes to Zuppa di Pesce "Ciambotto",* Vol. 83. $15
LORENZO DELBOCA, *Polentoni,* Vol. 82. Italian Studies, $15
SAMUEL GHELLI, *A Reference Grammar,* Vol. 81. Italian Language. $36
ROSS TALARICO, *Sled Run,* Vol. 80. Fiction. $15
FRED MISURELLA, *Only Sons,* Vol. 79. Fiction. $14
FRANK LENTRICCHIA, *The Portable Lentricchia,* Vol. 78. Fiction. $16
RICHARD VETERE, *The Other Colors in a Snow Storm,* Vol. 77. Poetry. $10
GARIBALDI LAPOLLA, *Fire in the Flesh,* Vol. 76 Fiction & Criticism. $25
GEORGE GUIDA, *The Pope Stories,* Vol. 75 Prose. $15
ROBERT VISCUSI, *Ellis Island,* Vol. 74. Poetry. $28
ELENA GIANINI BELOTTI, *The Bitter Taste of Strangers Bread,* Vol. 73, Fiction, $24
PINO APRILE, *Terroni,* Vol. 72, Italian Studies, $20
EMANUEL DI PASQUALE, *Harvest,* Vol. 71, Poetry, $10
ROBERT ZWEIG, *Return to Naples,* Vol. 70, Memoir, $16
AIROS & CAPPELLI, *Guido,* Vol. 69, Italian/American Studies, $12
FRED GARDAPHÉ, *Moustache Pete is Dead! Long Live Moustache Pete!,* Vol. 67, Literature/Oral History, $12
PAOLO RUFFILLI, *Dark Room/Camera oscura,* Vol. 66, Poetry, $11
HELEN BAROLINI, *Crossing the Alps,* Vol. 65, Fiction, $14
COSMO FERRARA, *Profiles of Italian Americans,* Vol. 64, Italian Americana, $16
GIL FAGIANI, *Chianti in Connecticut,* Vol. 63, Poetry, $10
BASSETTI & D'ACQUINO, *Italic Lessons,* Vol. 62, Italian/American Studies, $10
CAVALIERI & PASCARELLI, Eds., *The Poet's Cookbook,* Vol. 61, Poetry/Recipes, $12
EMANUEL DI PASQUALE, *Siciliana,* Vol. 60, Poetry, $8

Bordighera Press is an imprint of Bordighera, Incorporated, an independently owned not-for-profit scholarly organization that has no legal affiliation with the University of Central Florida or with The John D. Calandra Italian American Institute, Queens College/CUNY.

NATALIA COSTA, Ed., *Bufalini*, Vol. 59, Poetry. $18.
RICHARD VETERE, *Baroque*, Vol. 58, Fiction. $18.
LEWIS TURCO, *La Famiglia/The Family*, Vol. 57, Memoir, $15
NICK JAMES MILETI, *The Unscrupulous*, Vol. 56, Humanities, $20
BASSETTI, ACCOLLA, D'AQUINO, *Italici: An Encounter with Piero Bassetti*, Vol. 55, Italian Studies, $8
GIOSE RIMANELLI, *The Three-legged One*, Vol. 54, Fiction, $15
CHARLES KLOPP, *Bele Antiche Stòrie*, Vol. 53, Criticism, $25
JOSEPH RICAPITO, *Second Wave*, Vol. 52, Poetry, $12
GARY MORMINO, *Italians in Florida*, Vol. 51, History, $15
GIANFRANCO ANGELUCCI, *Federico F.*, Vol. 50, Fiction, $15
ANTHONY VALERIO, *The Little Sailor*, Vol. 49, Memoir, $9
ROSS TALARICO, *The Reptilian Interludes*, Vol. 48, Poetry, $15
RACHEL GUIDO DE VRIES, *Teeny Tiny Tino's Fishing Story*, Vol. 47, Children's Literature, $6
EMANUEL DI PASQUALE, *Writing Anew*, Vol. 46, Poetry, $15
MARIA FAMÀ, *Looking For Cover*, Vol. 45, Poetry, $12
ANTHONY VALERIO, *Toni Cade Bambara's One Sicilian Night*, Vol. 44, Poetry, $10
EMANUEL CARNEVALI, Dennis Barone, Ed., *Furnished Rooms*, Vol. 43, Poetry, $14
BRENT ADKINS, et al., *Shifting Borders, Negotiating Places*, Vol. 42, Proceedings, $18
GEORGE GUIDA, *Low Italian*, Vol. 41, Poetry, $11
GARDAPHÈ, GIORDANO, TAMBURRI, *Introducing Italian Americana*, Vol. 40, Italian/American Studies, $10
DANIELA GIOSEFFI, *Blood Autumn/Autunno di sangue*, Vol. 39, Poetry, $15/$25
FRED MISURELLA, *Lies to Live by*, Vol. 38, Stories, $15
STEVEN BELLUSCIO, *Constructing a Bibliography*, Vol. 37, Italian Americana, $15
ANTHONY JULIAN TAMBURRI, Ed., *Italian Cultural Studies 2002*, Vol. 36, Essays, $18
BEA TUSIANI, *con amore*, Vol. 35, Memoir, $19
FLAVIA BRIZIO-SKOV, Ed., *Reconstructing Societies in the Aftermath of War*, Vol. 34, History, $30
TAMBURRI, et al., Eds., *Italian Cultural Studies 2001*, Vol. 33, Essays, $18
ELIZABETH G. MESSINA, Ed., *In Our Own Voices*, Vol. 32, Italian/American Studies, $25
STANISLAO G. PUGLIESE, *Desperate Inscriptions*, Vol. 31, History, $12
HOSTERT & TAMBURRI, Eds., *Screening Ethnicity*, Vol. 30, Italian/American Culture, $25
G. PARATI & B. LAWTON, Eds., *Italian Cultural Studies*, Vol. 29, Essays, $18
HELEN BAROLINI, *More Italian Hours*, Vol. 28, Fiction, $16
FRANCO NASI, Ed., *Intorno alla Via Emilia*, Vol. 27, Culture, $16
ARTHUR L. CLEMENTS, *The Book of Madness & Love*, Vol. 26, Poetry, $10
JOHN CASEY, et al., *Imagining Humanity*, Vol. 25, Interdisciplinary Studies, $18
ROBERT LIMA, *Sardinia/Sardegna*, Vol. 24, Poetry, $10
DANIELA GIOSEFFI, *Going On*, Vol. 23, Poetry, $10
ROSS TALARICO, *The Journey Home*, Vol. 22, Poetry, $12
EMANUEL DI PASQUALE, *The Silver Lake Love Poems*, Vol. 21, Poetry, $7
JOSEPH TUSIANI, *Ethnicity*, Vol. 20, Poetry, $12
JENNIFER LAGIER, *Second Class Citizen*, Vol. 19, Poetry, $8
FELIX STEFANILE, *The Country of Absence*, Vol. 18, Poetry, $9
PHILIP CANNISTRARO, *Blackshirts*, Vol. 17, History, $12
LUIGI RUSTICHELLI, Ed., *Seminario sul racconto*, Vol. 16, Narrative, $10
LEWIS TURCO, *Shaking the Family Tree*, Vol. 15, Memoirs, $9
LUIGI RUSTICHELLI, Ed., *Seminario sulla drammaturgia*, Vol. 14, Theater/Essays, $10
FRED GARDAPHÈ, *Moustache Pete is Dead! Long Live Moustache Pete!*, Vol. 13, Oral Literature, $10

JONE GAILLARD CORSI, *Il libretto d'autore, 1860–1930*, Vol. 12, Criticism, $17
HELEN BAROLINI, *Chiaroscuro: Essays of Identity*, Vol. 11, Essays, $15
PICARAZZI & FEINSTEIN, Eds., *An African Harlequin in Milan*, Vol. 10, Theater/Essays, $15
JOSEPH RICAPITO, *Florentine Streets & Other Poems*, Vol. 9, Poetry, $9
FRED MISURELLA, *Short Time*, Vol. 8, Novella, $7
NED CONDINI, *Quartettsatz*, Vol. 7, Poetry, $7
ANTHONY JULIAN TAMBURRI, Ed., *Fuori: Essays by Italian/American Lesbians and Gays*, Vol. 6, Essays, $10
ANTONIO GRAMSCI, P. Verdicchio, Trans. & Intro. , *The Southern Question*, Vol. 5, Social Criticism, $5
DANIELA GIOSEFFI, *Word Wounds & Water Flowers*, Vol. 4, Poetry, $8
WILEY FEINSTEIN, *Humility's Deceit: Calvino Reading Ariosto Reading Calvino*, Vol. 3, Criticism, $10
PAOLO A. GIORDANO, Ed., *Joseph Tusiani: Poet, Translator, Humanist*, Vol. 2, Criticism, $25
ROBERT VISCUSI, *Oration Upon the Most Recent Death of Christopher Columbus*, Vol. 1, Poetry, $3

www.ingramcontent.com/pod-product-compliance
Lightning Source LLC
Chambersburg PA
CBHW031843220426
43663CB00006B/483